OUR
WORLD
OF
SCIENCE

OUR WORLD OF SCIENCE

By Duane Bradley
and Eugene Lord

ILLUSTRATED BY
TIBOR TORS

J. B. Lippincott Company

PHILADELPHIA AND NEW YORK

CONTENTS

OUR WORLD OF SCIENCE

Introduction

DID YOU EVER watch a television program with the sound turned off? Even though you could see the picture clearly, you could not follow the story very well. Without being able to hear, you missed most of what was going on.

When you hear the word *Science* you may think it sounds dull, or like something too hard for you to understand.

This is really not true at all. Science is just the name we give to learning about our world. The more we know about our world, the more exciting it is to live.

Knowing more about our world is like having both a picture and sound on television. The more we know about science, the more interesting everything becomes. Without science, life is like a television picture without sound.

Scientists are people who know a great deal more about things than we do, but science itself is something that all of us can learn.

Our world is full of puzzles, and from the time we can talk, we ask questions. We want to know how and why and when and where.

Science is learning the answers to these questions. If you like to ask questions and find out the answers, you may want to be a scientist when you are grown. Even if you do not decide to be a scientist, you will enjoy learning what science can tell you about our world.

There are new words in science, because science is learning about new things. Meeting a new word is like seeing someone you never saw before. At first his face will look different to you, but when you get to know him he will soon become a friend. The words science uses are not hard to understand, and very soon they will become your friends.

It is always more fun to do things than to read about them, so this book is full of things to do. The things that we do in science are called "experiments." (That's one of the new words.) An experiment is something you do to find out what will happen.

All of the experiments in this book can be done with things you have, or can get very easily. You can do them by yourself, or with a teacher. They are easy to do, and safe, and very interesting. Each one of them will answer a question or tell you something new about the world in which you live.

When you read this book and do the experiments, it will be like visiting a new and exciting land. It is not really a new place, but a new way of seeing the world about you.

We have had fun planning your trip for you, and we hope you have a wonderful time!

Duane Bradley
Eugene Lord

1. The World of Air

WE LIVE at the bottom of an ocean of air.

Can you imagine walking around on the bottom of an ocean of air? Air is much lighter than water, and we cannot see it, but the ocean of air is much larger than any ocean of water on our earth.

Do you know how far a mile is? Our ocean of air reaches three HUNDRED miles into the sky.

You do not notice the weight of air, as you would feel the weight of water if you were under it, but it is really quite heavy. You have weighed yourself on a scale and watched the hand on the dial move to a number that tells you how heavy you are. Did you ever put one foot on a scale and push as hard as you could, to see how high the hand would go? You were pressing down with your foot, or using pressure. When you weigh yourself on a scale, the hand on the dial shows how much pressure, or weight, your body has.

When we talk about the weight of the air, we call it "air pressure." Air presses down on the earth, and on us, just as you press on a scale when you weigh yourself.

You cannot feel the air pressing on you, but it is there all the time. Look at the picture which shows a square inch. Then look at the back of your hand. Are there about four square inches of skin there? The pressure of air on EVERY square inch of your body is about fifteen pounds.

There are so many square inches of skin on the outside of your body that you are "carrying" almost thirteen TONS of air-weight pressure all of the time. An automobile

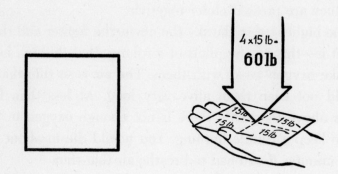

weighs only two or three tons, and you certainly could not lift one—but you are always being squeezed by that much weight of air.

If someone dropped thirteen tons of something on top of you, you would be mashed flat. How can you be strong enough to carry thirteen tons of air pressure all the time?

Air is really very light, compared to other things in our world. It is because there is so much of it that it weighs so much. One cubic foot of air all by itself weighs only one and a quarter ounces—but think how many cubic feet of air there are in our ocean of air! Think of the air, for a moment, as a tall pile of pillows. Each pillow is quite light, but each one presses down on the one beneath it, so that a pile of them can be very heavy.

Did you ever sit on a pillow and flatten it? The air at the bottom of our ocean of air is pressed down by all the air above it so that it is much "denser" than the air higher up. This lower air is like the pillow that is flattened by weight —the pillow contains just as many feathers as it did before, but they are pressed closer together.

The higher up in the sky the air is, the lighter and thinner it is—this is why pilots of airplanes that fly high have to take oxygen tanks with them. The air is so thin that it would not keep them alive very long. At less than five miles above the earth, there is not enough oxygen in the air to keep a candle burning. You would die in about fifteen minutes if you had to breathe air that thin.

Way down at the bottom of our ocean of air, where we are, the air is dense, and the air pressure is heavy. Yet we walk and run and play and never feel this weight that is pressing down on us. Why is that?

Our bodies are built to live in our world. Inside our bodies are different pressures that help us stand the weight of air without noticing it. If you push against someone who is smaller and weaker than you, he will fall down. If you push against someone your size who is pushing back, he will not fall down. The pressures in our body push back against the pressure of the air so that we cannot even tell it is there.

We say that the air is "transparent," which means that it is so clear we can see through it. Did you know that something you cannot see at all can be made up of many different things? These things in the air are called "gases."

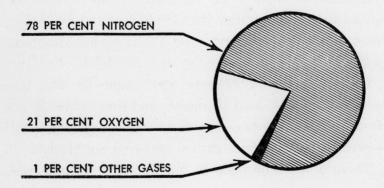

78 PER CENT NITROGEN

21 PER CENT OXYGEN

1 PER CENT OTHER GASES

You have probably taken a toy to pieces to see what it was made of. Scientists have taken air to pieces to see what it is made of.

If you change a dollar into pennies, you will have one hundred pennies. If you could divide a piece of air up into one hundred parts, you could get a good idea of the amounts of the different gases that make it up. Seventy-eight of the hundred parts of the air are nitrogen; twenty-one of them are oxygen. This leaves only one other part— and this part contains the other gases.

The names of the gases in the air seem very strange, but there is a reason for them. When someone discovers something no one knew about before, it has to have a name. Usually the name chosen is one that seems to fit. When the gas we call Argon was discovered, it seemed to be a very lazy gas that did nothing, so it was named a word that means "won't work."

Helium was found in the sun before it was found in our air, so it was named after the Greek word for sun, *helios*. Neon means "the new one," and Xenon means "the stranger."

Oxygen isn't really a very good name for that gas, because it means "acid producer" and some acids do not contain oxygen. Carbon came from a word meaning "coal" —perhaps because both carbon and coal are black.

There is more nitrogen in our air than anything else.

Nitrogen is a slow, lazy gas that does very little. Oxygen is one of the most important gases in the air. There is much less of it than of nitrogen, but it does a great deal more. Do you know someone who always wants to be a part of everything that is going on? You can think of oxygen that way—in science, we say that it unites with many different things.

When oxygen unites very fast with something, it causes what we call fire. When a piece of wood burns, flame and smoke appear, and we say that the wood is burning. Although it may seem to, the wood does not disappear, or vanish, but changes into ashes and gases. We can see the ashes, but the gases mix with the air. In our world, many things which seem to vanish do not really disappear but change into something else.

Sometimes oxygen unites more slowly with something, and no smoke or flame can be seen. Whatever it unites with changes slowly into something else. This is another kind of burning.

Did you know that there are very, very tiny "fires" in your body all of the time? This is what keeps you warm.

When you breathe air into your lungs, the oxygen passes through very small openings in the "membranes" of the air sacs in your lungs. It goes through these openings into your blood.

The blood carries the oxygen to the cells of your body. These cells are so small that they can be seen only under a microscope. At the same time, the food you eat is being digested in your stomach and intestines so that very small bits of it (they could only be seen under a microscope, too) can be carried by the blood to the cells of your body.

When the food particles and the oxygen meet in the cells, the oxygen unites with the food. This causes a kind of burning and gives off the heat which keeps you warm.

Air is one of the most changeable things in our world. Sometimes it is moist, and sometimes it is dry. Sometimes it is hot, and sometimes it is cold. Sometimes it seems to be very still, and other times it moves so fast we say the wind is blowing.

Air can change its size quickly. When it grows, or gets larger, it also gets thinner so that it weighs less. Here is something else very strange about air. Air can become moist, which means that it contains water vapor. If you filled a sponge with water, it would weigh more than when it was dry. When the air contains water vapor, it is lighter than when it is dry.

When we talk about "air pressure" we are talking about the weight of the air above us. When air is warm and moist and weighs less, we say it has "low pressure." When it is cool and dry and weighs more, we say it has "high pressure." When you listen to a weather broadcast on the radio or television, you may hear something about low pressure areas and high pressure areas. This means places where the air is light, and places where it is heavy.

An odd thing about air is that it is almost impossible to make a hole in it. A hole in the air means a place where there isn't any air—or anything else. This is called a "vacuum." Did you ever throw a rock into a pool of water, and see how quickly the water closes? You can't make a hole in water, and it is quite difficult to make a hole in the air.

If you have a glass full of water, you can pour the water out of it—but you can't pour air out of a glass. When air moves from one place to another, more air rushes in to fill the space. There are vacuums, or holes, in the air and you can probably see one in the room where you are. Is there a light bulb near you? The air has been forced from the light bulb, and the bulb sealed so that no air can get back in.

Sometimes holes in the air are made by different things —but the hole closes quickly, and we hear a loud noise. Lightning makes a hole in the air, and when the air rushes in to fill it up, we hear the noise of thunder. If you have ever broken a light bulb and heard the pop, it was the sound of air rushing in to fill the hole.

As you can see, air is one of the strangest and most interesting things in our world.

Because it can do so many different things, and change in so many ways, there are many experiments you can do with it.

Here are some of them:

AIR CAN BURN STEEL

Steel is very strong, but you can make it burn.

You will need a drinking glass, a piece of steel wool, (your mother may have some in the kitchen that she uses as a scouring pad, or your father may have some in his workshop), and a shallow pan, like a pie tin.

Put some water in the pie tin. Wet the steel wool and push it tightly into the bottom of the glass. Turn the glass upside down and set it in the pan of water.

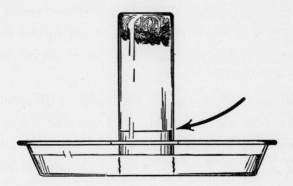

In a few days you will see something very strange happening.

The steel wool is turning a different color, and very slowly getting smaller. The water is getting higher in the glass. What is happening?

The steel wool is slowly being burned. There is no smoke or flame, and very little heat. The steel is not turning to ashes, as wood or paper does when it burns, but into rust.

The oxygen in the air has united with the steel, making it burn. If you leave it long enough, the steel will disappear and only rust will be left.

We wet the steel wool for this experiment because the water acts as a "helper." Metal which is damp will rust much faster than dry metal.

Many metals "burn" like this when they are exposed to air. Whenever you see rust on metal, it is "burning." This is why metal is painted or covered with oil or grease so that it will last. The paint or oil or grease keeps the oxygen away from the metal and protects it against burning.

Why is the water getting higher in the glass? When the oxygen united with the steel, it left the air—and air does not like empty spaces. The rest of the air in the glass spread out to fill the inside of the glass, which made it thinner. As you know, thin air has less pressure than dense air. The air outside the glass had more pressure than the thinner air inside, so it pushed the water up inside the glass.

This experiment can be done in a different way with special equipment and is very exciting. If a piece of steel is heated red hot and put into a container of pure oxygen it will burst into flame. In our experiment the air does not contain enough oxygen for this to happen, so the burning takes much longer.

You Can Pick up Water with a Drinking Straw

Would you think that something with a hole in the bottom would hold water?

A drinking straw has a hole at each end, but you can fill it full of water and carry it without spilling, without closing the hole in the bottom.

You will need a drinking straw and a tall thin bottle. An olive bottle will do nicely.

Fill the bottle with water and put the straw into it. You will see that the water in the straw rises as high as the water in the bottle.

Now put your finger over the top end of the straw. Hold it there while you take the straw out of the bottle. The water stays in the straw. It will stay there as long as your finger covers the top end of the straw.

Why does this happen?

As we saw before, there is air almost everywhere in our world. When something is moved from one place to another, air rushes in to fill the empty space.

This works the other way, too. Sometimes things cannot be emptied unless there is a way for air to get in and fill the space that would be left. If air could get in the bottom end of the straw the water could run out—but the bottom end is so small it is like a one-way street. The water is blocking the street, and no air can get past it.

As soon as you take your finger off the top end, air rushes in, and the water runs out.

Here is another way to see how this works.

Take the bottle in which you filled the straw and pour out the water. Air rushes in the opening of the bottle and fills the space left by the water. Fill a large pan full of water and put the bottle in it. When the bottle is full of water, turn it upside down (be careful to keep the top opening under water as you do this) and slowly raise it to the top of the water. As long as this opening is under water so that no air can get in, the water will stay in the bottle. The second you raise the mouth of the bottle even a tiny bit above the water, air will come in and the water will pour out.

Did you ever open a can of fruit juice or milk? You always punch two holes in the top—one for the air to come

in, and the other for the liquid to rush out. When your mother opens a can of cranberry jelly, she punches a hole in the bottom of the can, and then takes off the top with a can opener—for the same reason.

This is the reason it is so hard to get tomato catchup out of a small-necked bottle—there isn't enough room for air to get in so the catchup will run out.

The Magic Glass

This looks more like a magic trick than a scientific experiment.

You will need a drinking glass and a sheet of thin smooth paper, large enough to cover the mouth of the glass.

Work over the sink the first time you do this, but after you have practiced you can do it safely anywhere.

Fill the glass with water to the brim. Put the piece of paper over the top of the glass—very smoothly. Be sure there are no wrinkles in the paper, especially on the edge of the glass.

Hold the paper in place, and turn the glass upside down. The water will stay in the glass. It will stay there until the paper becomes wet and rips, or until it wrinkles around the rim of the glass.

What holds the water in the glass?

Before you read this paragraph, think about the drinking

straw experiment, and see if you know the answer. It is the same thing at work here—air pressure. The water cannot leave the glass until air can get in to take its place. Even the thinnest piece of paper will keep air out, and keep the water in the glass.

You Can Blow up a Balloon with a Milk Bottle

If someone told you that, you wouldn't believe it, would you?

This is what you will need—a milk bottle, a balloon, a saucepan, and your mother's stove.

Put some water in the saucepan. Stretch the end of the balloon over the mouth of the milk bottle. Set the milk bottle in the pan, and the pan on the stove. Heat the water slowly. As the water gets hot, the balloon is blown up.

What happened?

You know that there was air inside the milk bottle, and now there is air inside the balloon. There is still air inside the milk bottle, so where did the air come from that blew up the balloon?

One of the strange things about air is the way it expands. To expand means to get bigger. Air does not get bigger the way you do as you grow, but by spreading out to take up more space. As you get bigger, there is more of you. When air expands, there is no more air, but it is spread out more thinly.

Air is made of gases, and these gases are made of molecules. Molecules are very, very tiny, and they are almost always moving.

Did you ever see a colony of ants busy scurrying around on the ground? Think of something much smaller than ants (molecules are far too small for us to see them), but just as busy moving.

When air is heated, the molecules quickly move farther apart, so that they take up more room. As they rush around they hit the walls of the container and create pressure.

If air were heated very hot inside a strong sealed container, the pressure caused by the molecules hitting the sides would make the container explode. The milk bottle is strong enough to hold the air (which does not get too hot in this experiment), but the balloon, being rubber, stretches from the pressure of the hot air.

If you take the bottle out of the water and let the air in the bottle cool, you will see the balloon slowly go down to its original size. This is because the molecules have gotten closer together and do not take up so much room.

You Can Use Air Pressure to Break Rubber

This looks like the experiment you just did, only backward. Instead of blowing up a balloon, you are going to use a milk bottle to break a piece of rubber from a balloon.

The odd thing about this experiment is that what seems to happen is not what happens at all.

You will need a milk bottle, some rubber from a balloon, a rubber band, and a pan.

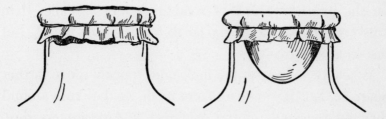

Put just enough water into the milk bottle to cover the bottom. Put the bottle in the pan of water, and put the pan on the stove. Heat it slowly until the water in the pan begins to boil. Now VERY CAREFULLY take the bottle from the pan (use a pot holder, so you won't get burnt). Stretch the rubber over the top of the bottle and fasten it on with the elastic band. Now watch what happens!

The rubber is drawn inside the bottle, and after a while it breaks with a snap! Why?

It looks as if the rubber were pulled into the bottle, but it was really broken by a push. Air expands as it warms, and as it expanded it went out of the mouth of the milk bottle. The water that was in the milk bottle turned into water vapor as it got hot, and filled the space left by the air that went out. It also pushed out more air, because water vapor fills a great deal of space. One cubic inch of water, turned into vapor, will make about one cubic foot of water vapor.

You ALMOST made a vacuum inside the milk bottle. So much air left during the heating that the bottle was nearly empty. The rubber stretched over the top of the bottle kept air from getting in. As the water vapor inside the bottle cooled, it got smaller. It turned into liquid water again, which takes much less space. The air also took less space as it cooled.

The air outside the bottle had much more pressure than the air inside. It pushed hard against the rubber, trying to fill the low pressure space inside. This is what broke the rubber.

Did you ever use a straw to drink? Most of us think we are pulling the drink up through the straw, but we aren't. We pull air from the straw, leaving an empty space. The drink is pushed in to fill this empty space by the pressure of the air outside.

You Can Starve Fire

People, plants and animals need oxygen in order to live. So does fire.

This experiment looks simple, but a number of exciting things are happening.

You will need a short candle, a saucer, and a tall glass.

Set the candle in the saucer. You can light the candle and let some of the melted wax drip onto the saucer. Set the candle in the soft wax, let it harden, and it will hold the candle in place. Now light the candle and watch it for a minute.

Set the glass over the candle, and you will see the flame go out almost at once.

What happened?

In your experiment with "burning" steel wool, you saw that oxygen can unite with steel and slowly change it to rust. In this experiment, oxygen was uniting with two different things. A candle flame is not as simple as it seems.

All fuels that we use for fire contain two important things —carbon and hydrogen. Oxygen, as usual, united with both of these. When it united with carbon, it made two other gases—carbon monoxide (which made the flame) and carbon dioxide, which was given off into the air.

When it united with hydrogen, it formed water vapor, which mixed with the air. These fire-making changes need a very large supply of oxygen. There was not enough oxygen inside the glass to keep the fire alive very long.

If you want to see this work more slowly, put a short candle inside a drinking glass and light it. Take a piece of cardboard, and slide it slowly over the top of the glass. As the top of the glass is covered, the flame will begin to flicker—if you pull the cardboard away, the flame will start to burn brightly again. You can see what happens as the flame starves.

The next time you look at a candle flame, or at a fire, think of all the things that are happening as it burns, and all of the changes that are taking place.

You Can Make a Fire Extinguisher

You have seen a fire extinguisher, but did you ever wonder how one worked?

You will need a short candle, a drinking glass, one-half teaspoon of baking soda, and a few drops of vinegar. Set the candle inside the glass (use melted wax to hold it in place, just as you did before), and pour an inch of water into the glass.

Put the soda into the water, and stir with a spoon handle or drinking straw until it is dissolved. Light the candle.

Now pour a few drops of vinegar at a time into the soda-water combination. Watch what happens!

When you have added just enough vinegar, the flame of the candle will go out, though you have seen nothing touch it!

What happened?

It seems hard to believe that baking soda contains carbon and oxygen, but it does. When an acid is added to some things which contain carbon and oxygen in just the right combination, another gas, called carbon dioxide, is formed. Vinegar is an acid—when it was added to the soda, carbon dioxide was quickly formed. The bubbles that you saw were made by this action.

Carbon dioxide is a heavy gas. It does not burn, and it does not give oxygen to help other things burn.

As the carbon dioxide escaped from the vinegar-soda mixture, it rose around the candle flame and held off the air, which contains oxygen. In a way, it made a wall around the flame and kept the oxygen out. It starved the flame, just as you did when you covered a burning candle with a glass.

Here is something odd—carbon dioxide is so heavy that you can pour it. If you will pour the liquid out of the glass, the carbon dioxide will pour out with it—and you can relight the candle.

A Lamp Can Turn a Pinwheel

Did you ever make a pinwheel spin by blowing on it? Perhaps you have put one on the front of your bike, or held one out of a car window, to make it turn.

You know that it takes moving air to do the job—but did you know that heated air is usually moving?

You will need a pinwheel made of a four-inch square of writing paper, a pin, some sticky tape, and a regular table lamp.

Make your pinwheel as shown in the diagram. Turn the corners as shown, and pin them in place with the pin. Now turn the pinwheel over and with tape attach a piece of thread to the pointed end of the pin.

Turn on the table lamp and hold the pinwheel over it. Soon it begins to turn. Why?

The lamp is not blowing on the pinwheel—or is it? Take the pinwheel away for a minute and hold your hand above the lamp. Can you feel the heat?

Warm air is lighter than cold air. The air in the room is not very cold, but it is cooler than the air just above the lamp.

The air in the room seems to be very still, but whenever

air is of different temperatures, it is moving. Warm air, being lighter than cold air, spreads out and moves upward. Cold air moves in to take its place, and makes the warm air move upward faster. If this movement were very fast, you would call it a wind—it is hardly enough for you to feel it, but it is enough to make the pinwheel turn.

You can prove to yourself how warm air acts by doing this simple experiment. First, put your hand on the floor. Now stand on a chair, and put your hand as high in the air as you can. Do you notice how much warmer the air is near the ceiling?

Warm air is light, cold air is heavy. This keeps air in movement, and many interesting experiments can be done with moving air.

You Can Sail a Boat with a Candle

Do you have a sail boat that moves when the wind pushes on the sail? Would you like to make a sail boat that makes its own wind?

You will need some aluminum foil (or the metal foil from a candy wrapper), four bobby pins, some sticky tape, and a piece of very thin wood (like that from a strawberry box), about five inches long.

Cut a sail about three by four inches in size. Bend two of the bobby pins to form equal angles (see sketch) and bend the other two out straight. Fasten one bent bobby

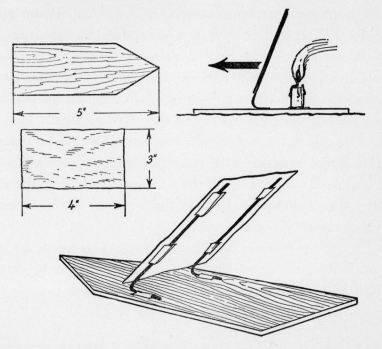

pin to a straight one with sticky tape, then do the same thing to the other two.

The foil is your sail—you will see how to fasten the bobby pins to it in the picture. Now fasten the other ends of the bobby pins to the boat with tape. The sail should be bent back so that the top is tipped about two inches toward the back of the boat.

Light the candle and find the best place to set it on the boat. It should be as near the sail as possible, but not close enough to overheat it. When you have found the right place, glue it there with melted wax.

Now set the boat in a pan of water (the bathtub is a good place, too) and light the candle.

Why does the boat sail?

You know that heat makes air move, and that this moving air can make other things move.

The heat from the candle makes currents of hot air rise and flow along the underside of the sail. The hot air is being pushed by the cold air around the candle, and the cold air gets hotter as it moves close to the candle. More cold air rushes in, gets warm, and moves on—this makes a constant motion in the air, which makes the boat move.

The Friendly Ping-pong Balls

Wouldn't you think that if you blew between two Ping-pong balls they would move apart?

Why don't you try it and see?

Take two pieces of thread the same length, and fasten each one to a Ping-pong ball with sticky tape. Hang the balls in a doorway, or some place where they can swing freely, so that they are an inch apart.

Blow through a drinking straw EXACTLY between the two balls. (If the stream of air is off to one side, this experiment won't work.)

Instead of flying apart, or going forward, the balls move toward each other. Why?

When air is moving fast, it has less pressure than still air. The air you blew through the straw was moving fast, so the pressure from the air on the outer sides of the balls was greater than the pressure of the air between them. This pushed the Ping-pong balls toward each other.

You can do this experiment with two Ping-pong balls floating on top of water. Put them about an inch apart, blow between them, and the same thing will happen.

The Cardboard that Sticks to a Spool

This seems like a bit of magic, and you might like to fool your friends with it.

You will need a spool (the kind that sewing thread comes on), a small nail, and a piece of cardboard.

Put the nail through the center of the cardboard, then drop the nail down the hole in the spool. This puts the cardboard flat against the end of the spool.

Hold it up in the air, hold the cardboard in place, and blow through the hole in the spool. You can let go of the cardboard at once, and the harder you blow the closer it will stick to the spool. You can even point the spool toward the floor, and as long as you keep blowing, the cardboard will stay in place.

Why?

You would think that you could blow the cardboard away from the end of the spool quite easily. It doesn't work that way.

When you blow through the spool, you make a current of moving air. The pressure in this air is less than the pressure of the air outside it. This current of moving air comes out in a thin, flat stream between the end of the spool and the piece of cardboard—the harder you blow, the less pressure there is in this stream of air. The less pressure

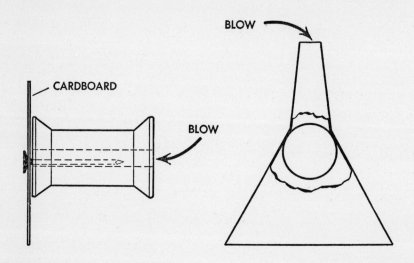

there is, the more the outside air pushes against the cardboard to hold it in place.

The Ball in the Magic Funnel

Here is another experiment with moving air that you might not believe unless you saw it.

You will need a small funnel (like those used to fill narrow-necked bottles), and a Ping-pong ball.

Hold the funnel upside down and put the Ping-pong ball inside it. Place the Ping-pong ball so that it covers the opening into the funnel. Now start to blow. Take your hand away from the ball, keep blowing, and the ball will stay inside the funnel.

You don't need to ask why this time. You already know.

2. The World of Water

Most of the outside of our world is covered with water. When we think about the world, we usually think of it as land with some water on it, but there is more water than land on the outside of our world.

Water is one of the important things that make up our world, and we call these things "matter." Matter is a very good word to use when you are talking about many different kinds of things.

Water, like other matter, is not always the same. Without changing into something else, it can change from one form to another. The three forms of water are liquid, solid and vapor.

We see liquid water fall from the sky as rain, we drink it, and we take baths and swim in it. We form solid water into balls and call them snowballs, or put another kind of solid water into drinks to cool them and call it ice. We never see water when it is vapor, but it is always in the air, and we breathe it all the time.

We say that water has three different forms, but is always water. This is because water does not change into something else, even when it changes in form and appearance and temperature.

Scientists say that water is H_2O. They are talking about what water is made of. They mean that when two hydrogen atoms and one oxygen atom are put together, they make water. Water can freeze into ice or become so hot that it is vapor, and it is still made of H_2O.

An atom is so small that if it were made two million times as large as it is, it would only be the size of a very small bit of sand.

Everything in our world is made of atoms. There are only ninety-two natural kinds of atoms, but they are mixed in many, many different ways to make different things.

This is how it happens. If your mother gave you a cup full of flour and told you to eat it, you would think she was teasing. If she mixes other things with the flour and bakes bread, you know that it is very good to eat.

The atoms in our world change just as much as that when they are put together in different ways.

Hydrogen and oxygen are both gases when they are atoms. When two atoms of hydrogen and one atom of oxygen are put together they make a special kind of molecule, called the water molecule.

When water changes from frozen ice to liquid to vapor, the water molecule stays just the same. Scientists can put the right atoms together to make water, and they can divide water back into these atoms.

When water changes from one form to another, it is because it is getting either hotter or colder. Water molecules, like good friends, cling together. They are always moving around, but sometimes they move faster than at others. When water is heated, the molecules move very fast, and get farther apart. Some of them go so far that they leave the liquid water and go into the air. They have become water vapor, which is a gas. If water is heated enough, all of it will go into the air as vapor, and we say that it has evaporated. If you will break the word into pieces, like this, e-vapor-ated, you will see why we use that word.

When water becomes cooler, the molecules move more slowly, and get closer together. The water gets thicker and as it gets still colder, turns into solid water, or ice or snow.

All matter in our world does this same thing. Some kinds of matter are almost always in one form, so we think of them that way, but they can change. A stone is really frozen rock and it must be made very hot in order to melt into a liquid, but it can be done.

Did you ever hear rain water called fresh water? We can say it is fresh because the molecules that make it have just joined together in large enough drops to fall. On the other hand, we can say that the molecules themselves may be thousands of years old.

There are always molecules of water vapor in air. They are light, so they are carried upward. As they go up they get into cooler air. Cool air is not so friendly to water vapor. It says, "Get out—no room for you here!" The water molecules that are pushed out of cool air rush together. When enough of them are close to each other, they form very, very tiny balls of water. These balls are like the steam you see coming from boiling water. When they are in the sky, they are clouds.

As the water molecules get into still colder air, they join together in larger drops. Soon the drops are heavier than the air, so they begin to fall to the ground. This is what we call rain.

If the drops of water fall through a place where the air is very cold, they freeze into sleet. If they are blown high above the earth into still colder air, they turn into hailstones. Sometimes water molecules get into air so cold that they freeze before they can join together. Then they fall as snowflakes.

One of the queerest things about water is that it gets larger when it gets very hot, and it also gets larger when it is very cold. Most forms of matter are smaller when they are "frozen," or solid, and larger when they are heated. This is one of the puzzles about water that you may solve some day, because no one is sure of the reason now. You can see this for yourself by watching how pans boil over as the liquid in them gets very hot, and also noticing that when ice cubes freeze in a tray, they take up more space than the water from which they were made.

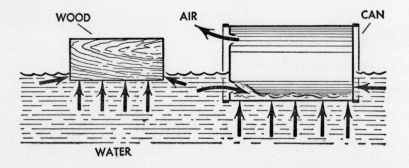

Water, like air, has pressure because of its weight. If you fill a can with water, you can tell that the weight of the water is pressing on the bottom of the can. If you put a small piece of wood in the water, you can tell that water presses upward and holds the wood on top. If you punch a hole in the side of the can, you can see by the way the water pours out that it is also pressing against the sides of the can. Water presses in all directions.

If you fill a glass with water and let it stand on a level surface until it is very still, you will not see any difference between the top of the water and the rest. There IS a difference—the top layer of molecules on the surface of water cling together tightly and form what is called "surface tension." Tension means "being pulled." These molecules pull on each other, and are pulled downward by the water molecules beneath them. They are not pulled as hard by the air molecules above them, so they form something like a very thin, elastic skin.

Here are a few experiments to show you some strange things about water:

You Can See What Happens When Molecules Move

You will need a glass, a few drops of ink or vegetable coloring, a saucer, and a small pan.

Fill the glass almost full of water. Let it stand until the water is still. Now carefully drop one or two drops of ink or other coloring into the glass. (If you do not have an eye dropper, you can use a straw. Remember the way you held water in a straw in the chapter on air?)

The coloring stays in one spot for only a very short time. Then it begins to move and makes beautiful patterns in the water. If it is left long enough, all of the water becomes the same color, and you can no longer see the coloring you dropped in.

Why?

The molecules of liquids are always in motion, even in liquids that seem to be quite still. The molecules of the coloring are moving, and are moved by the water molecules. When the water is evenly colored, you can no longer see anything happening, but the molecules are still moving.

For your second experiment, pour a fourth of a cup of

water into the pan, and put it on the stove. Heat it slowly, and watch the water turn into steam. Remember that steam is not water vapor, but water molecules that have come into cooler air and joined together to make tiny, tiny drops. You cannot see water vapor. Look at the space between the top of the water, and the steam. That is where the water vapor is.

Very soon the water is gone, and the pan is empty.

What happened to the water?

Molecules in heated water move more rapidly than those in cool water. As they move they get farther apart. When water is heated very hot, the molecules move so fast and so far that all of them go into the air as water vapor.

Did you ever see the windows in a room where there was a great deal of hot water become covered with steam? Sometimes this happens in a bathroom, if someone takes a very hot bath. The water vapor that went into the air cooled when it touched the window glass, and made steam.

For the third experiment, put a fourth of a cup of water in a saucer. Mark the saucer to show where the water reaches. Set the saucer on a window sill, or in a warm place.

This experiment takes longer than the one with water that is heated in a pan, but the same thing happens. The water in the saucer gets lower and lower, day by day, until finally the saucer is dry.

Water evaporates as water molecules go into the air,

even if the water is not very warm. When the water is spread out thinly it evaporates faster than when it is in something like a bottle with a narrow neck. Wherever water touches air it makes a "door" through which the molecules can get out of the water. The larger the door, the faster the water evaporates.

The Diving Bottle

You will need to be as careful and exact as a real scientist, and you may have to try many times before you get this experiment right.

You need a milk bottle, a very small bottle (like a pill bottle), and a piece of rubber from a broken balloon.

Fill the milk bottle with water. Now fill the pill bottle about one-quarter full of water.

Put your finger tightly over the top of the pill bottle, turn it upside down, and quickly put the open end down in the milk bottle.

If you have just the right amount of water in the pill bottle, it will float almost under the water in the milk bottle. If it sinks, take it out and empty a drop or two of the water, and try again. If it seems too light, add a drop or two of water.

When you have the pill bottle floating just right, add enough water to the milk bottle to replace what you splashed out. Do this carefully, so you won't upset the pill bottle.

Now, if you touch the pill bottle very gently, it will sink to the bottom of the milk bottle, and then slowly rise to the surface.

Place the palm of your hand over the top of the milk bottle and press down. The pill bottle will sink, and slowly rise to the surface again.

Put a thin piece of rubber (from a balloon) over the top of the milk bottle and fasten it with a rubber band. You can now make the bottle sink by pushing on the rubber. By experimenting, you can learn to push just hard enough to make the pill bottle float anywhere you want it to in the water.

This is what happens when you make the bottle sink; you are changing the volume of air inside the small bottle.

The air in the pill bottle is lighter than water, which lets the bottle float. When you press on the rubber stretched over the mouth of the milk bottle, this pressure is carried through the water into the air in the pill bottle.

This pressure on the air inside the pill bottle compresses it so that it takes up less space. Water from the milk bottle is pushed into the pill bottle by this same pressure and makes up for the difference in the air volume. The pill bottle, with more water added to it, weighs more. It sinks.

When you stop pressing on the rubber, there is no extra pressure to be carried to the air in the small bottle. It returns to its original volume, the water goes back into the milk bottle. The pill bottle is again as light as it was before, and floats.

WHY THINGS FLOAT

We can stop things from going down toward the earth if we can push them upward strongly enough. When things stay on the top of water instead of sinking to the bottom, we say that they are floating.

Things float on water because the water is pushing them up just as hard as they are being pushed down by their weight. Light materials, like wood and paper, will float on water very easily. When they become soaked with water so that they are heavier, they sink.

We know that this is true. We also know that most

metals, like steel and iron, are much heavier than water.

Why do we make our great ocean liners out of metals, and why do they float when what they are made of is heavier than water? Here is how you can answer this question:

You will need a piece of aluminum foil and a pan of water. First, shape the aluminum foil like a dish, with a bottom as flat as you can make it, and the edges bent up to make sides. Put it on top of the water. It floats very easily.

Now crumple it up in your hand into the shape of a ball. Put it on the water and it will sink. The aluminum foil did not get heavier, so why did it sink?

When the aluminum foil was made into a dish, its bottom was large enough to give the water several square inches to push against. When the whole upward push of the water was as great as the whole downward pressure of the foil, the foil floated. It was actually held between the two pressures when they became equal.

When the foil was crumpled into a ball, there was much less surface, so the upward push against it was much less. This is why huge ocean liners that weigh so very much can float on deep water.

Lighter Liquids Will Float on Heavier Ones

There are many different liquids in our world, and some of them are much heavier than others. Oil looks as if it would be heavier than water, and you can find out whether it is or not.

You will need a small round bottle, some cooking oil, and some coloring (like that Mother uses for cake icing).

Fill the bottle about three-quarters full of water. Add a few drops of coloring, and shake it until it is all the same color.

Now pour a little bit of cooking oil into the bottle.

The oil does not sink to the bottom, but floats. It is lighter than water!

If you want to see something interesting, put a top on the bottle, and shake it. The oil goes down through the water, and then floats back to the top. Did you notice that it forms tiny balls of different sizes as it goes into the water? Later we will see why this happens.

The Mystery of Surface Tension

Molecules of water attract each other. Each one pulls on all of the others, and this pull is called "cohesion."

When water is quiet in a bowl, the molecules that are on the very top pull on each other and on the ones below. They are pulled on by those below, but not by the air molecules above them. All of this pull makes the top surface of water like a very, very, thin elastic skin.

As thin as it is, it is amazingly strong.

Floating Steel on Water

You will need a sewing needle and a bowl of water.

Rub the needle with your fingers. The oil from your

skin will make the needle slightly oily. Oil molecules, like air molecules, do not pull on water.

Let the water in the bowl become quiet. Hold the needle with your thumb and finger and set it very lightly on top of the water. It will float.

Now push down on one end of the needle. It is just as if the needle had punctured the surface tension, and broken it. It sinks to the bottom at once.

You rubbed the needle with your fingers to make it oily to keep the water from clinging to it. Oil and water do not mix. The oil on the needle kept the water molecules from clinging to the needle and climbing up its sides. Molecules of different things have a certain attraction for each other, which is called "adhesion."

If you will look closely, you can see that the water in the bowl curves up slightly at the edges. This is caused by adhesion, which lets the water molecules climb up a little way on the glass.

You can see something else interesting about surface tension if you will fill a glass full of water to the brim. Now add more water, just a drop at a time. If you do this carefully, the water will rise a bit above the top of the glass, so that the glass is a little more than full. Surface tension keeps it in place.

WATER MOLECULES MAKE THINGS MOVE

You will need a pie plate, a candle, and a cube of sugar.

Scrape very fine particles of wax from the candle and scatter them on top of the water. Touch the water with one edge of the cube of sugar. The bits of wax move toward the sugar.

The cube of sugar looks solid, but it is porous, or full of tiny holes. When it touches liquid, the water molecules rush into these holes because of the attraction of adhesion. The sugar acts like a blotter, which soaks up liquid.

When the water molecules rushed into the sugar, their motion moved the bits of wax.

Now scrape a tiny bit of soap onto the tip of a toothpick, and dip that into the water. The bits of wax move away from the soap.

The minute you put the soap into the water, small bits of soap went into the water. The part of the water with soap in it had its surface tension weakened at once. The rest of the water had a much stronger surface tension. The wax was pulled away from the soapy area by the greater pull of the surface tension.

To do this experiment in a different way sprinkle talcum powder over the top of a shallow pan of water. Touch the center of the talcum powder with the edge of a wet cake of soap.

Almost at once the talcum powder rushes away from the soap and makes a round clear place around it.

A Boat that Is Moved by Surface Tension

You will need a thin narrow piece of wood, like the flat stick from a popsicle. Or you can cut it from the wood of a berry box.

Make the piece of wood about an inch long, and cut one end to a point. Make a small notch in the center of the other end. Stick a small piece of wet soap into the notch.

Set your "soap boat" in a pan of water. It begins to move forward at once. It will keep going for quite a long time.

What do you think makes it go?
It is cohesion and adhesion at work.

When water molecules touch a surface that will become wet by them, they cling to that surface by adhesion. This force, and the force of surface tension, cause the water to curve upward where it touches the edges of the boat.

This stretches the surface of the water, because the force of adhesion is pulling a little stronger than the cohesion of the water molecules are pulling on each other.

If the soap were not on the boat, it would be pulled on evenly in all directions, and would stay in one place.

The soap, though, dissolves in the water. This weakens the surface tension there. This means that the forces pulling on the front of the boat are stronger, and so the boat is pulled forward by them. It looks as if the boat is being pushed by the soap, but it is really being pulled. If you will think about the experiment with the soap and the bits of wax on water, you will see that this is another way of using one of the laws of our world.

Why Water Makes Drops

Did you ever notice that rain drops look like balls with a point on one side? Did you ever splash water and see how it forms into drops as it flies through the air?

When water is in a glass or a pond or a bathtub, it takes the shape of whatever holds it. That is because the force of whatever is holding water is pressing in into that shape.

When water is "free," or not being pushed or pulled by

any outside force, it takes a different form. This is always the form of a sphere, or ball.

The outside molecules of water, as we know, are pulled by cohesion toward each other. When water is free, surface tension pulls it into the shape of a sphere.

When you poured oil on top of water and shook it, you saw that the drops of oil took the shape of spheres or balls as they rose through the water. This was surface tension at work. The oil rose to the top because it was lighter, or had less density, than water.

When a liquid is suspended or floats in another liquid which has the same density, this strange action can be seen plainly.

You will need a tall narrow bottle, enough water to fill it half full, and as much rubbing alcohol as water. You will also need a few drops of cooking oil.

Fill the bottle half full of water. Add rubbing alcohol very slowly by pouring it down the side of the bottle. You do not want the alcohol and water to become completely mixed. Be careful not to stir or shake the bottle.

At some point in the bottle, this mixture of alcohol and water will have the same density as cooking oil.

Put some cooking oil into the eye dropper. Very carefully lower the end of the dropper about an inch or two into the water. Put just one drop of oil into the water. It will float, or be suspended, at the exact place where the density of the water-alcohol is just that of the cooking oil. The oil will make a perfect sphere.

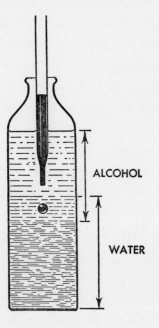

ALCOHOL

WATER

Do not worry it you cannot do these experiments perfectly the first time. They will all work, so keep trying. Scientists learn to be patient and to try and try again until they have done an experiment perfectly.

It is surface tension which makes drops of water take the shape of a sphere. If you take a piece of modeling clay and flatten it out, it will have more outside surface than if you roll it into a ball. Any kind of matter, shaped into a ball, has less outside surface than in any other shape.

As drops of water move freely, either through the air, or suspended in a heavier liquid, they take the shape of spheres. This is because the pull of surface tension brings the outside molecules as close to each other as they can get. This makes the water into the shape which has the least amount of surface area and is called the "shrinking" action of surface tension.

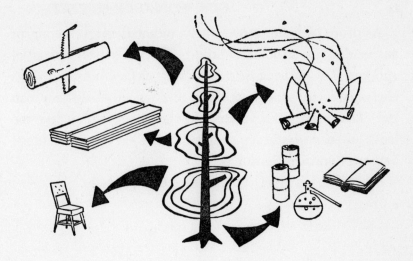

3. The World of Change

NOTHING in our world is ever lost, but everything in our world is always changing. We can see some of these changes, as we see tiny seeds start to grow in the spring and become big plants by summer. All of us have seen kittens grow into cats, and clouds turn into rain that falls, and mud dry out and turn to dust. Other changes take so long that we do not notice them happening.

When a tree in a forest is cut down and sawed into lumber in a mill, it is changed. Some of it is made into boards, and some of it turns into sawdust. The sawdust and the boards are still wood—the tree has made what we call a "physical change." Its form and appearance are different, but it is still wood.

If we take a piece of wood and put it on a fire and burn it up, it has changed in a different way. It is no longer wood, but ashes, soot, smoke and gases. This kind of change is called a "chemical change." The molecules which made wood have changed into molecules which make other things.

One way that things change is when they "dissolve." If you put a spoonful of sugar into a cup of water, you can stir it until the sugar seems to be gone. If you taste the water, you can tell that the sugar is still there, because the water is sweet.

The molecules of sugar moved away from each other and scattered evenly through the water. You saw this same thing happen when you watched coloring spread through a glass of water. The sugar molecules are still sugar molecules, but they are spread out very thinly. You can take them back out of the water, and they will look like sugar again.

When something dissolves in a liquid, we call the liquid the "solvent" and the thing that dissolves the "solute."

Scientists call water the "universal solvent" because almost all forms of matter will dissolve in a certain amount of water.

When molecules of one substance spread out, they are moving. Nothing can move without energy or force to make it move. Heat is a kind of energy. The sugar dissolves in the water because the heat energy in the water makes the sugar molecules move out of the crystal form.

This sounds strange, when you know that sugar will dissolve in a cold drink like lemonade. How can it be true?

Even water that we call cold has some heat in it. If it did not, it would be frozen into ice. The hotter water is, the faster sugar will dissolve in it, because hot water has more heat energy.

When your father stirs sugar into his cup of coffee, the coffee gets a little cooler. Some of the heat energy in the coffee is used up by dissolving the sugar.

When salt is dissolved in water it makes the water act differently. Salt water has to be heated more than plain water before it will boil. It has to be colder than plain water before it will freeze.

If you live in a part of the country where there is much snow in the winter, you may have seen highway trucks put salt on the snowy roads.

When alcohol is mixed with water, it can get very cold without freezing. In cold weather, we put some kind of alcohol in our car radiators to keep them from freezing. The water-alcohol mixture will boil at a lower temperature than plain water. Did you ever see clouds of steam coming from a car radiator? Probably it still had the winter "antifreeze" in it, and the car got so warm it began to boil.

Here is a puzzle about solutions. When a solute is dissolved in a solvent, the molecules of the solute have scattered into the spaces between the molecules of the solvent. If we put 5 teaspoons of sugar with 5 teaspoons of sand, we will have 10 teaspoons of the mixture. If we add 5 teaspoons of alcohol to 5 teaspoons of water, we have only 9 1/2 teaspoons of alcohol-water. If we add 5 teaspoons of ammonium chloride to 5 teaspoons of water, we have MORE than 10 teaspoons of the mixture. Maybe when you grow up, you will find out why this happens.

We can make another kind of change that looks like a solution, but is not. The matter mixed in a liquid goes into such tiny particles that it seems to be dissolved. These particles are "suspended" or "held" in the liquid. Muddy water is a good example of this. The mud seems to be part of the water, but if it stands still long enough it will sink to the bottom. The mud is still mud, but was only suspended in the water.

We can see the mud in the water, but another kind of "suspension" cannot be seen. This is when the particles of matter are so tiny they cannot be seen and the water looks quite clear. You can be a detective and spy out this kind of change by using a flashlight. A beam of light through what is called a "colloidal suspension" will show that something is in the liquid.

When ice melts into water, it "steals" heat. When you put ice cubes into lemonade to make it cooler, the ice steals the heat from the lemonade as it melts, and the lemonade gets colder.

When water changes into vapor, or evaporates, it also steals heat. Wet one finger and hold it up in a breeze. The part of the finger that gets cooler shows that the breeze is blowing from that direction. The breeze began to evaporate the moisture on the finger, and the skin got cooler.

When steam is cooled so that it turns into water, a great deal of heat is given off in the change. We use this to heat our homes in the winter, and call it "steam heat." The furnace changes hot water into steam, which goes into radiators. As it turns back to water in the radiators, the heat it gives off is enough to heat a room.

These are some of the ways in which things in our world change. Making changes and watching what happens is one of the most exciting things in science.

Here are some experiments in change that you can do:

Making Sugar Climb a String

You know how easy it is to stir sugar into water, but do you know how to get it out again?

You will need sugar, a glass or cup, a pencil, and a piece

of string. Add some of the sugar to the water and stir it
until it is dissolved. Keep adding sugar until no more will
dissolve. This is called a "saturate solution," which means
that the liquid is completely saturated with whatever is
dissolved in it. The liquid does not have any more room for
a solute.

Now tie the string around the center of the pencil and
lay the pencil over the top of the glass so that the string
hangs in the solution.

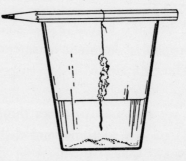

By the next day, you will see crystals of sugar on the
string. If you leave the string long enough, the sugar will
leave the water and climb the string. You will have a string
covered with frosty sugar crystals.

You can do this experiment with salt, too.

Another way to do it is to use a cup of very hot water.
Hot water will dissolve more sugar than cool water, and

as it cools you will see many more sugar crystals on the
string.

How to Make an Emulsion

An emulsion is a mixture in which one liquid is not dissolved, but is suspended in another. It is in very tiny particles that float inside the other liquid.

You will need one-quarter cup of dissolved soap and
one-half cup of kerosene. Cut the soap up into tiny pieces
and heat it slowly in one-quarter cup of water until thick.
(This is soft soap.)

Put the soap into the kerosene and shake it.

Each tiny droplet of kerosene is surrounded by a thin
film of soap. The droplets will stay suspended for a long
time.

This is why we use soap to clean things. Much of the
dirt on us, and on our clothing and dishes and pans, is
slightly oily. Soap, when dissolved in water, emulsifies
this oil, or surrounds it with a tiny film. These tiny bubbles
of oil and dirt can easily be washed away.

How a Change in Form Steals Heat

Did you ever wet your finger and hold it up in the air
to see which way the wind was blowing? When one side of
your finger felt colder than the other, you knew the wind
was coming from that direction.

The water on your finger changed its form as its molecules went into the air. Moving air helped them change their form more quickly. As they changed, the force that changed them stole heat from your finger. This made your finger feel cooler.

For this experiment, you will need two thermometers and a wet cloth. The cloth should be wet with water that has been standing long enough to be the same temperature as the air in the room.

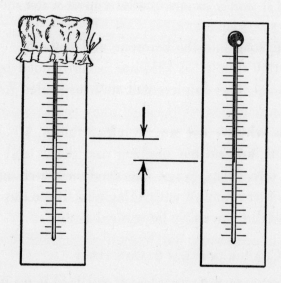

Look at the thermometers to see that they both show the same temperature. (If two thermometers in the same place don't show the same temperature, one of them is not working right.) Now put the wet cloth on the bulb of one thermometer, and see what happens. It shows a lower temperature than the other one.

You are using what weather forecasters call the "wet-bulb" and "dry-bulb" thermometers. By measuring the difference between the two temperatures shown, they can tell how much moisture is in the air. If the wet bulb thermometer is much lower than the other, it shows that the air is very dry and the water on the cloth is evaporating quickly. If the temperatures stay the same, it shows that the air is so wet it cannot hold any more water.

Using Light as a Detective

What scientists call a colloidal suspension often looks like a solution. This is because some things go into such very tiny particles that they seem to be dissolved, although they are still themselves and not part of the solvent.

When scientists are experimenting, they often make control tests, to be sure of what is happening. Would you like to try that?

You will need some starch, some sugar, milk, water, two glasses, and a flashlight.

First, stir sugar into a glass of water. Flash a beam of light through this solution.

Now add enough milk to a glass of water to color the water slightly. Flash the beam of the flashlight through this.

Now empty the first glass, and stir some starch into water until it seems to be dissolved. Flash the beam from your flashlight through this. In this last experiment, you see something different. Where the light goes through the water, you see a milky streak. This is the very tiny particles of starch that are suspended, but not dissolved, in the water.

Your flashlight has detected a colloidal suspension that you could not see with your eyes.

Did you ever see a beam of sunlight from a window that made this kind of streak in the air? The beam of light showed very tiny dust particles suspended in the air.

How to Clean Pennies

When pennies are first made, they are bright and shiny. After a while they become old and dark-looking. You can make old pennies look as bright as new.

You will need some old pennies, vinegar, salt, and a shallow bowl.

Pour the vinegar into the bowl and stir salt into it to make a thin paste. Put the pennies into this mixture.

Very soon they begin to lose their dark coats and become shiny.

This experiment shows us that chemicals are not just things that scientists use, but are part of our everyday life.

Vinegar is about five per cent acetic acid. When salt is

mixed with it, it forms a weak hydrochloric acid. This acid will dissolve copper oxide, which is the tarnish found on pennies.

The Mysterious Moth Balls

For this experiment you will need moth balls, one-quarter glass of vinegar, and one-half teaspoon of baking soda, and a glass.

Put the vinegar in the glass, then add enough water to fill it. Add the soda, and stir slightly.

Now drop two or three moth balls into the glass. They sink to the bottom, then slowly rise to the top, then slowly sink to the bottom again. They will keep doing his for a long time.

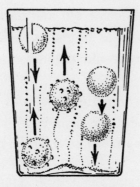

When soda is added to the vinegar-water solution, carbon dioxide gas is formed. The force of adhesion (the attraction between unlike molecules) makes the carbon dioxide gas cling to the moth balls. The carbon dioxide is lighter than water, and when enough of it is clinging to the moth balls, the moth balls become light enough to rise to the surface.

When the moth balls come to the top, the carbon dioxide gas bubbles burst and the gas goes into the air. The moth balls become heavy enough to sink again.

If you color the water blue, and use a glass bowl for this experiment, it is even prettier. You can do the same experiment with ginger ale instead of the soda and vinegar and water combination.

The Disappearing Blue

No one knows for sure just what happens to the blue in this experiment, but you can see it happen.

You will need one teaspoon of cornstarch, one-half glass of water, and a few drops of tincture of iodine.

Stir the cornstarch into the water. Set the glass in a pan of water and bring the water slowly to a boil on the stove.

Let the mixture cool. Add a few drops of tincture of iodine, and stir. The mixture will turn blue.

Put the glass back in the pan of water and heat it again as before. The color disappears. Let it cool, and it comes back again.

CHEMICAL DETECTIVES

We know that vinegar is acid, and that some things are just the opposite, or alkaline. Sometimes chemists want to know whether a certain substance is acid or alkaline. They use what is called "litmus paper" to find out.

You can make your own paper which will tell you the same thing.

You will need hot water, some strips of newspaper torn from the margin, and either one or several of the following: hollyhock flowers, red cabbage, rhubarb juice or cherry juice.

Crush the flowers, or cabbage, in hot water. The rhubarb or cherry juice can be used just as it is. Soak the strips of paper in the liquid, and then let them dry.

Now, if you put one of the strips of paper into a liquid you want to test, a change in color will show you whether it is acid or alkaline.

Most of these papers will turn blue or green in alkalies, and red in acids. Sometimes they are not exactly these colors, so you can set up your own tests to see what they will do. Make a solution of vinegar and water for acid, and soda and water for alkaline. Use one paper of each different kind in these mixtures, and you can tell what color it will turn when you test other mixtures.

A Chemical Garden

We think of things that are alive as growing, but some chemical changes look very much like growth. One of the most interesting of these is called a "chemical garden."

BE SURE TO WASH YOUR HANDS AFTER YOU HAVE MIXED THE THINGS LISTED BELOW. THE CHEMICALS YOU USE MIGHT DAMAGE YOUR SKIN OR MOUTH IF YOU DO NOT.

You will need a shallow dish, four tablespoons of table salt, four tablespoons of bluing, two tablespoons of Mercurochrome, and a lump of coke (or piece of brick or piece of coal.)

Put two tablespoons of salt, two tablespoons of bluing and two tablespoons of Mercurochrome in the dish. Put the lump of coke (or brick or coal) in the center. After an hour or two add the other two tablespoons of salt and of bluing.

Before very long you will see a strange chemical reaction taking place, and a beautiful garden will grow as you watch it.

You might be interested to know that chemists call salt sodium chloride and bluing ferric ferrocyanide, and that when put together they make ferrous chloride, which is the white crystals that you see, and also sodium ferrocyanide.

How to Make Inks for Writing Secrets

The ink that you buy is good for writing words that you want everyone to read. If you want to write secrets there are ways to make inks that only those who know the trick can read.

Here are some good ones to try:

You will need cornstarch, lemon juice, iodine, water, and paper.

First, make a milky mixture of cornstarch and water. When you write with this, it cannot be seen when it is dry. To read it, pour a solution of iodine and water over the writing. Your magic ink turns blue.

This ink will not work with some papers, because they will turn blue all over when you put the iodine-water solution on them. Test your paper before you use it.

You can write with lemon juice which disappears as soon as the juice dries. To read this ink, hold the paper close to a light bulb, and it will turn brown.

Another ink can be made by adding several drops of iodine to a cold mixture of starch and water. This makes a blue ink—but after a few weeks the color disappears, and what you have written is gone.

How to Take Fingerprints

Detectives often get fingerprints which help them solve crimes. Here is a way you can take fingerprints. You will need a paper which will turn blue when an iodine-water solution is poured over it, (some typing paper will do this, since it is treated with starch when it is made) iodine, and Vaseline.

Mix enough iodine in water to make a tea-colored solution. (You can use this to test your paper. Put a drop of it on different papers, and choose the one that turns blue.)

Grease your fingerprints lightly with Vaseline, and press them gently on the paper for a few seconds.

Now pour the iodine solution on the paper. The fingerprints will be clearly outlined.

How to Put an Egg in a Milk Bottle

You will need an egg, vinegar, and a milk bottle. The neck of the milk bottle is much smaller than the egg, but you can make the egg go through it.

Put the egg in a teacup and cover it with vinegar. Let it soak until the shell becomes soft—like a rubber ball. If you check it from time to time you will see that the shell is becoming softer. When it is soft enough you can push it gently through the neck of the milk bottle.

The shell of an egg is mostly calcium carbonate. The acetic acid in vinegar makes a chemical change by which

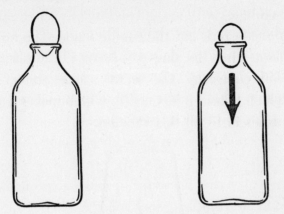

the hard calcium carbonate is partly destroyed, so the shell becomes soft.

How to Change Air

This experiment is quite simple to do, but a number of things happen almost at once.

You will need a tin pie plate, a short candle, water, and a drinking glass.

Set the candle in the pie tin, pour about three-quarters of an inch of water in the tin. Light the candle, and set the drinking glass over it.

What you see is the water rising about one-fifth of the way up the glass.

This is part of what happens: The candle flame is a combination of carbon, hydrogen and oxygen molecules. The oxygen in the air combines with carbon in the flame, which makes carbon dioxide, and also carbon monoxide. The hydrogen combines with oxygen and makes water vapor. The carbon dioxide puts out the candle flame. The air, heated by the flame while the glass was being put in place, is now cooler and contracts. The water vapor condenses into liquid, which takes up less space, which makes a vacuum. Water rushes in to fill this vacuum.

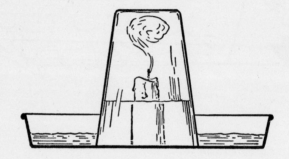

4. The World of Motion

Our world is always moving, and many things in our world move. Everything that moves must be started by a pull or push.

Things are pulled or pushed by what we call force. If you put this book down on the table, you will be using the force of your muscles. When your car goes down the road, the force of the fuel it burns is making it move. The clouds that float in the sky are moved by the force of air currents or wind.

Things that are not acted on by force do not move.

If you put a rock down on the ground, it would stay there forever unless it was acted on by force. If the rain fell hard enough to move it, that would be force, or if someone kicked it, that would be force.

Small things can be moved by very little force, but large heavy things need much more force to be moved.

It sounds very simple to say that nothing moves unless it is acted on by force. It is really one of the most important discoveries made by science.

Until we knew why things moved, we could not make cars go or airplanes fly. Think of all of the things in our world that move, and then ask yourself what moves each of them.

When a leaf turns color in the fall and becomes dry, it moves from the tree to the ground. Why does it move downward, instead of flying up out of sight? We know that the air above us is always in motion, and a leaf is so light that a little breeze will carry it.

If you look at the ground, you can't see anything pulling on the leaf. Why do leaves, and apples, and nuts, and everything that falls, always fall to the ground?

One of the most mysterious things in our world is a force called gravity. This force has always been here, ever since the world was made, and it is always acting on everything on the outside of our world. If you want to see it work, just pick up something and drop it. Gravity will pull it toward the ground.

When you throw a ball, it begins to curve down toward the ground the minute it leaves your hand. The stronger you are, the farther you can throw a ball. You act on the ball with force when you throw it. Gravity acts on the ball with a force that pulls it down.

Think of force as the push you gave the ball to make it move. This force would make the ball move in a straight line forever if it were not for gravity and air resistance. The force of gravity never stops, but keeps pulling downward as the ball travels, and finally pulls it to the earth.

Gravity is always pulling everything on the earth downward toward the center of the earth. The gravity of our earth can be thought of as an invisible blanket reaching out into space.

Our universe is made up of stars, planets, moons, the earth, and endless space. Each of these bodies has its own gravity which pulls on each other body. The larger a body is, the greater the pull of its gravity, but the farther away it is, the less its pull.

Our earth goes around the sun. This is because the sun is so much larger and its gravity is stronger than ours. The moon goes around the earth, because the earth is heavier than the moon, and its gravity is stronger.

We may think of our universe as many kinds of bodies of

different sizes. Each of these is pulling all the others with the force of gravity. These pulls have kept the bodies in our universe in the same paths of motion throughout time.

Another force is at work in our world and in our universe. This would seem to be the opposite of force, and we call it "inertia." The word "inert" means not moving, and inertia comes from that.

Science calls the facts that we know about motion "laws," and one of them is the law of inertia. This says that a body not acted on by a force will not move, and that a body set in motion by force will tend to move in the same direction at the same speed forever unless stopped by some force.

If you throw a ball, it goes in a straight line ahead of you. It does not turn to one side or the other, unless it hits something or is blown by the wind.

Inertia is the other force which keeps our universe in the same motion. Our earth started revolving around the sun a long time ago. It keeps revolving in the same line around the sun, and just the same distance from the sun. Inertia keeps it moving, gravity keeps it the same distance from the sun. If you want to see how this works, tie a pebble on a piece of string. Swing the pebble around your head. Think of your head as the sun, and the pebble as the earth. The force you put into swinging the pebble would make it go away from you in a straight line because of inertia, but the string, like the pull of gravity, keeps it just a certain distance from your head.

If it were not for inertia trying to keep the earth on a straight path, it would fall into the sun. If it were not for the gravity of the sun, the earth would take a straight path and fly off into space.

These are the things scientists knew when they got ready to put the first satellite into orbit around the earth. They knew that it had to be moved by a force strong enough to reach a spot hundreds of miles above the earth. They knew that it had to move at a speed of about 18,000 miles an hour to travel in a circle nearly 9,000 miles in diameter around the earth, 500 miles up in the air. The force of gravity in space is so small that the first satellite went all the way around the earth once every one and a half hours for about three months.

Another law of motion seems hard to believe. This law is that for every action, there is an equal and opposite reaction. This means that every time force moves something forward, another force just as strong goes just the other way.

Do you want to prove this? Touch the table very gently with your hand. Now hit the table harder. When you touch the table very gently, you can barely feel it. When you hit the table hard, you can feel it just as hard.

Did you ever see someone fire a big gun? The force of the powder that exploded in the bullet sent the bullet forward. The reaction from this force jerked the gun backward.

Did you ever blow up a balloon and then let go of it and watch it move through the air? The air inside the balloon pushed against the balloon, and could only get out through the open end. As the air came out the open end, it made a force. The reaction to this force made the balloon move in the other direction.

If you have ever seen a picture of one of our big rockets or jet planes in action, you may have seen something that looked like fire coming out of the tail end.

Inside the rocket is a fuel which burns so fast it acts like a powerful explosion. The force of this explosion-like fire can only escape through an opening in the back. The reaction to this force sends a rocket or jet plane through the air.

In the last few years, men have traveled faster than ever before. In your lifetime, they have learned to fly faster than sound can travel. Every year we learn new ways to go even faster.

Before we could do this, men had to understand motion, inertia and action-reaction. Here are some experiments that will help you understand them. When you do them, remember that these are the first steps on the way to the moon.

The Lazy Marble

Inertia makes things tend to stay where they are. This is a kind of force, although it seems to be no force at all.

For this experiment, you will need a card from a deck of playing cards, a marble, and a drinking glass.

Put the card on top of the glass, and put the marble in the middle of the card.

Now snap the edge of the card with your finger, hard enough to make it fly off the glass.

The marble falls into the glass.

You moved the card with the force of your finger. The force of inertia on the marble kept it from moving. The heavier anything is, the stronger the force of inertia that acts on it. The marble was so heavy that it was not moved when you snapped the card. Instead, it stayed where it was, and so fell into the glass.

When the card went out from under the marble, the force of gravity worked against the force of inertia, and pulled the marble down.

Inertia Acts Like Glue

Inertia can make an object stick to something else as if it were glued.

Get a wooden coat hanger with a flat wooden bar across the bottom, and a dime.

First put the dime on the wooden crossbar, and turn the coat hanger upside down. The dime falls off. This isn't surprising, you knew it would.

Now put the dime back on the crossbar, and swing the coat hanger by your finger in a circle, as fast as you can. As you swing the coat hanger, it is up side down part of the time, but the dime stays where it is.

Perhaps you have done the same thing with a pail of water. If you swing the pail in a circle, the water does not spill.

This seems as if it breaks the law of gravity, but it doesn't. It shows us another force which can be stronger than gravity as long as it lasts. We call this "centrifugal force."

When the dime was put in motion, it had a strong urge to go in a straight line. Since the coat hanger was going in a circle, it was carried in the same circle. Because of its urge to go straight, it pushed harder and harder against the coat hanger, and this kept it in place.

The dime on the crossbar was held in place by the force

of inertia, and stayed there as long as the coat hanger turned rapidly in a circle.

THE STRETCHING CIRCLE

You will need a long piece of thin rubber (from an extra-big rubber band), and a small pebble.

Tie the pebble to one end of the rubber band. Swing it around your head in a circle.

Notice that the faster you swing it, the more it stretches. As it stretches, the circle it makes becomes bigger and bigger.

When you swung a pebble tied to a string around your head, the string could not stretch. The rubber band can stretch, and the faster you swing it, the stronger the pull of the pebble gets.

When you put the pebble into motion, it would have gone in a straight line unless it was held by the rubber band. The force of inertia pulled it outward, but your pull on the other end of the rubber band kept it "in orbit," or going in a circle.

As you swung it faster, it pulled even harder away from you, and this pull made the circle of its path larger.

WHY A COWBOY'S LARIAT MAKES A CIRCLE

Did you ever watch a cowboy do tricks with a lariat? He held one end of the rope and the loop at the other end made a perfect circle as he swung it. Perhaps you have tried to do this, and found that it was difficult. Cowboys have learned the trick of handling a lariat, but you can see the law of our world that makes this happen.

You will need an egg beater, a pencil, and a short piece of small strong fishline.

Tie one end of the fishline to one of the bottom blades of the egg beater. Be sure your knot isn't going to rub against the beater anywhere, because the egg beater needs to turn fast to do this.

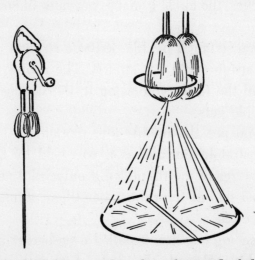

Tie one end of the pencil to the other end of the fishline.

Now stand up and turn the egg beater as fast as you can. The fishline begins to spin around, and as it does the pencil lies flat in the air and turns in a circle.

Why doesn't it just hang down and spin as the line spins?

This is the action of inertia when an object rotates, or turns, around a center of gravity. Did you ever seesaw? The seesaw is balanced on its center of gravity, so both ends move up and down freely. Did you ever balance a pencil on your finger? When it balances, it is resting on its center of gravity. The center of gravity is also the point around which an object will rotate smoothly.

The cowboy's lariat does the same thing. When the rope is spinning properly, the loop on the end takes the form of a spinning circle.

If you hang a loop of chain on the end of the fishline in this experiment, it will spin in a circle.

The Moving Dime

You can make a dime move without touching it because of the laws of inertia and motion.

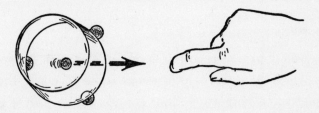

You will need a drinking glass, three pennies, and a dime. Your working surface must be a table with a cloth on it.

Rest the glass, bottom up, on top of the three pennies,

and put the dime under the center of the glass. With your fingernail, begin scratching the tablecloth toward you about two or three inches from the dime. Each time you scratch, the dime moves toward you, though you have not touched it.

The first time you scratched, you moved the tablecloth forward a tiny bit. This motion was a slow steady pull, which overcame inertia better than a quick jerk. It started the dime moving with it. The dime, once set in motion, continued to move forward a little as the cloth snapped back in place between scratches.

The glass on the pennies, of course, was too heavy to be moved by this amount of force.

Here is the law of inertia. "All bodies in the universe are in a state of rest or uniform motion in a straight line unless some external force changes that state." Have these experiments shown you what that means?

Force that Goes Two Ways

The law of action-reaction is one of the most interesting in our world. It says that for every force forward, there is an equal force backward. This sounds funny, but it really works.

You will need a toy wind-up car, a square of cardboard for the car to sit on, and two round pencils.

Set the cardboard on the two pencils, and put the wind-up car on the cardboard. Wind up the car, and let it start forward. As its motor sends it forward, the cardboard goes backward.

The force that moves the car forward is accompanied by an opposite force, or reaction. This reaction makes the cardboard go backward.

If the wind-up car were on the table, or on the ground, the force of reaction would not move the table or ground enough to be seen.

The Box that Comes Back

When you do this experiment, you will be making a toy. Perhaps you already have a toy that is called a "comeback." This experiment will make another one, and tell you how it works.

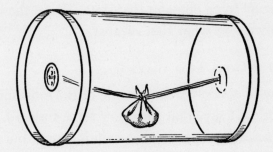

Get a round cardboard box, like a pint ice-cream container, a piece of cardboard, an elastic band, a square of thin cloth, and some pebbles.

Put a handful of pebbles inside the square of cloth, then

tie the corners together so it makes a bag. Tie the bag of pebbles in the center of the rubber band. Make a slit in the center of each end of the cardboard box. Make cardboard buttons like those shown. Put the loop ends of the rubber band through the holes in the ends of the box and over the buttons, as shown.

Roll the box across the floor. It rolls away, stops, and then rolls back toward you.

This is what happens inside the box: As you roll it, the bag of pebbles is so heavy it hangs without turning. The rolling motion winds the rubber band. When the box stops, the rubber band begins to unwind, and the force from the unwinding motion brings the box back.

Your wind-up toys work in very much the same way. When you turn the key to wind them, you are tightening a spring inside. In a way, you are putting the force into the spring. As the spring uncoils, the force is used to make the car go.

The Wonderful Soo-Soo Stick

Here is a toy you can make that will amaze your friends. You will know how it works, but they will think it is almost magic.

You will need a short round wooden stick (a wooden dowel or a rod from your Tinker Toy set), a straight pin, a piece of stiff cardboard, and a smaller wooden stick (a pencil will do for this one).

Cut notches almost halfway to the center of the first stick, in a straight line. Cut a propeller from the stiff cardboard, and fasten it to one end of the stick with the straight pin.

Now take the pencil and rub one edge of it rapidly along one side of the row of notches, back and forth. As you do, the propeller will begin to spin.

Rub the pencil along the other side of the row of notches and the propeller will begin to spin in the opposite direction.

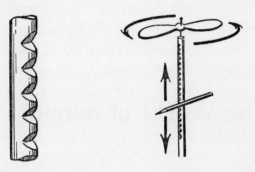

As you rub the edge of the pencil over one side of the row of notches, the stick vibrates. It does not vibrate straight up and down, but in a rotary, or circular, path. This is because each notch that the pencil strikes turns the motion of the stick in a curved path. As this continues, the circular pattern of vibration is carried to the propeller, which begins to spin.

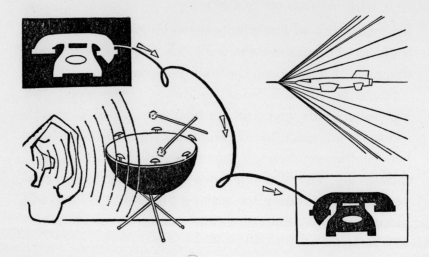

5. The World of Sound

Sʜᴜᴛ your eyes for a moment. What do you hear?

Our world is full of sound—soft sounds, loud sounds, faint sounds and harsh sounds.

The odd thing is that all of these sounds are in your ears. If we had no ears, our world would be silent. What MAKES sound would still be here, but it is our ears that turn it into sound.

Did you ever walk into a room that was completely dark? As far as your eyes could tell, there was nothing in

the room but you. The minute the light was turned on, you
could see the furniture, the walls, the windows, and everything else that had been there all the time.

Sound is like that. Sound is always in the world, but
without our ears we could not hear it.

Sounds are made by vibrations. If you will hold a rubber band loosely between two fingers and pull it sharply,
then let go, you will see it move back and forth. The rubber band is vibrating, or making vibrations. If you will
pull the rubber band tighter and pull on it, the vibrations
will be faster, and it will make a noise.

Vibrations make sound waves. When these sound waves
reach our ears, they are turned into what we call sound.
We might say that our ears are like radios which receive
sound waves and turn them into something we can hear.

Did you ever throw a rock into water, and watch the
circles spread out from the spot where it hit? When the
stone struck the water, it put the water into motion. This
motion was carried as waves through the water.

A leaf on the water would move up and down as the
waves passed, but would not be carried along by the wave.
This shows that only the waves are moving. The water is
not moving over the surface. A sound wave does not
move the air, but moves through the air.

This is hard to imagine, but think of it this way: the outside of each sound wave is a layer of compressed air. This
means that the particles of that air are moved closer to-

gether by the force of the sound. This force, or compression, moves from one part of the air to another, but the air does not move with it. Just as the leaf moves up and down on the water, but does not go with the wave, the air particles are compressed and released by the passing of the sound wave, but stay where they are.

When a body vibrates rapidly in the air, sound waves move out from that point. (Do you remember that we said the word body in science means an object, or a thing?) Sound waves are more like bubbles than circles. Each vibration makes a "bubble" of sound, one inside the other, all moving outward at a great speed. In one second the surface of a sound bubble moves eleven hundred feet from the starting point.

Some sounds are high, like a whistle, and some are low, like a bass drum. The difference is caused by the speed with which vibrations are made.

Put a yardstick on a table so that one end extends about two feet beyond the edge of the table. Hold the end on the table firmly. Tap the overhanging end. The yardstick vibrates back and forth, but you do not hear anything. You have caused vibration, but no sound. Can this be true?

Do you have a radio set that will get more stations at night than in the daytime? All of the stations are broadcasting in the daytime, but your radio station cannot get them then.

Our ears cannot hear all of the sound in our world. Most of us cannot hear sounds that are caused by vibrations slower than 16 each second. Most of us cannot hear vibrations of more than 16,000 per second. The number of vibrations per second is called the "frequency," so our sound range is between a frequency of 16 vibrations per second and 16,000 vibrations per second. That still leaves a great deal of sound for us to hear.

If you move the yardstick so that only a foot extends from the table, and flick the end again, you will hear a sound. The vibrations are faster, and the noise has come within your sound range. If you do this experiment several times, and shorten the amount of yardstick that extends from the table, you can make different sounds. The shorter the length, the higher the sound will be. Did you notice that when the yardstick vibrated fast enough so that you could hear it, you could no longer see the vibrations? When a vibrating object looks blurred to us, it is making sound waves fast enough for us to hear.

Animals hear sounds that we cannot hear. Did you ever see a "silent" dog whistle? It makes a sound so high that we cannot hear, but that dogs hear easily.

Bats hear sounds up to 50,000 vibrations per second. This helps them "see" with their ears. As they fly through what seems complete darkness to us, they make a very high sound. The sound waves they send off are "bounced" back to them by objects in their path. When you are walking and see a tree ahead, your eyes tell you it is there, so you do not run into it. When the bat flies toward something his ears tell him it is there so he can dodge it.

What the bat hears is called an echo. When sound waves hit something hard, they are bounced back as echoes. Echoes are not as loud as the sound that made them, because some of the energy of the sound wave is absorbed by the surface. When sound waves hit soft surfaces, their energy is almost all absorbed.

In radio broadcasting stations, echoes are not wanted. The walls of broadcasting studios are made of materials that absorb the energy of sound.

Have you ever walked into an empty room and noticed how odd your voice sounded? That was because there was little in the room to absorb the energy of the sound waves. Furniture, people, curtains—all of these things in a room absorb sound-wave energy.

Sound is one of the fastest things in our world. It travels about a mile in five seconds. It travels faster when the air is warmer, and slower when the air is cooler.

One reason that airplanes go faster than boats is that boats travel in water. Water is thicker than air and slows the speed of the boat.

But with sound it is different. It can travel fifteen times faster through steel than through air, and four times faster through water than through air.

Men were very proud when they built the first airplane that could travel faster than sound. The newspapers were full of stories about airplanes that "broke the sound barrier."

When we say "barrier" we usually mean something solid and heavy. If you build a dam in a stream, you have made a barrier to keep the water from flowing. How can anything that we cannot see, and that travels as fast as sound, make a barrier?

You must use your imagination to understand this. Think of a large jet motor on an airplane. This jet motor makes a very loud noise when it starts. Huge bubbles of sound go out around the point where they are started. As the airplane travels, the sound waves go out in all direc-

tions around it, one sound bubble inside another. These sound bubbles are traveling outward one mile every five seconds.

The surface of each sound bubble is a layer of compressed air. Inside this is a layer of thin air. Compressed air, you remember, is packed more tightly together than thin air.

If you will draw a picture of an airplane inside sound waves you can see this. Draw a circle around the airplane, then a larger circle around that, then a larger one, and so on until you have a dozen or so circles, each larger than the next.

With the real airplane, there are hundreds of these circles, and more being made each instant. Each circle moves out and gets larger all the time as sound comes from the jet motor.

The real airplane is not standing still, but moving. It goes faster and faster, until it is going faster than the sound bubbles. The instant this happens, it has caught up with the sound waves, and broken through all of those layers of compressed air.

Terrific shock waves are made, just as if a huge wave in the ocean crashed against a stone wall. Often what we call a "sonic boom" is heard for miles around. Sometimes, when the sonic boom is heard, windows in houses miles away are broken.

Can sound waves break glass? If they can, why aren't

all the windows in the world broken, when there is so much sound in our world?

The answer is strange. Vibrations cause sound, and sound can cause vibrations. Every object in the world has a "natural frequency of vibration." This means that if sound waves of the right vibration touch an object with the same vibration frequency, they will make it vibrate. This does not happen very often, but if you watch for it you may see it.

Sometimes a note struck on a piano will make forks and spoons on a table vibrate. Some singers can hit a certain note and make drinking glasses vibrate.

When things vibrate long enough, they break.

Did you ever see soldiers marching, each one in perfect step with the other? If a large group of soldiers march over a bridge, each keeping step with another, they may start the bridge vibrating. If the vibration is strong enough and lasts too long, the bridge may break, even though it is very strong. It would not break if heavy trucks, that weighed more than the soldiers, drove over it. Soldiers who march over a bridge are told to get out of step until they are on the other side, so this will not happen.

Science now uses the vibration caused by sound to do many things. They work with what we call "ultrasonic" frequency, which means sound waves higher than we can hear. These ultrasonic vibrations can be used to kill germs, and even to kill small animals.

There is still much for us to learn about sound. Do you want to start by doing these experiments?

Why You Have Two Ears

To do this experiment you will need two pennies, a friend, and a blindfold. Tell your friend that you can prove to him that he can't tell you where sound comes from.

Blindfold him, and hold one penny with the edge between your thumb and forefinger, the other penny with its edge between your forefinger and second finger. By pushing the first penny against the other with your thumb, you can make a clicking sound.

Click the pennies under the bottom of the center of his chin and ask him where the sound came from.

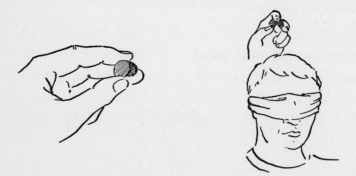

Click them in the center of the back of his head, and ask him again. You can click them in front, behind or on top of his head as long as it is exactly between his two ears. He won't be able to tell you where the sound is coming from.

We don't know exactly how our ears tell us from what direction a sound comes. Sound travels so fast that it is hard to believe our brains can tell the difference in time between the instant that it strikes one ear and the other. It is just as hard to believe that the difference in loudness between the six inches or so that separates our ears can be told. However, in some way our ears, set on each side of our head, can tell the direction of sound.

Just between our ears is a line in which our ears cannot find the source of sound because it is not closer to either ear. When we are blindfolded, any noise from this line can fool us.

How to Hear Cathedral Bells

Sound travels better through a solid than through the air. Because of this, there is a surprising difference in sounds.

Tie a silver spoon to the center of a piece of string. Hold one end of the string to each ear, and ask your friend to tap the spoon.

What you hear sounds like cathedral bells. Now take the ends of the string from your ears and have your friend tap the spoon again. The sound waves, traveling through air to reach your ears, sound entirely different. Now let your friend try it.

How to Make a Telephone

Get two tin cans or round cardboard boxes (like ice cream or cereal boxes), a friend, two toothpicks, and a long piece of string.

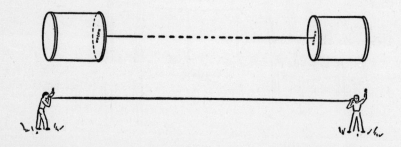

Punch a small hole in the center of the bottom of each can or cardboard box. Put the string through these holes, tying each end to a toothpick to hold it in place.

Give your friend one "phone" and you take the other. Walk as far apart as you can, keeping the string tight and straight between you. Now if you whisper into your phone and your friend holds his phone to his ear, he can hear you. The sound waves are traveling through the string.

The Swinging Ping-Pong Balls

You can make a Ping-pong ball swing without touching it. Cut a piece of string in three parts—two 2 feet long and one 3 feet long. Fasten each of the two even lengths to each of the Ping-pong balls. (Use sticky tape for this.) Now tie the other ends of these strings to the longer string, about one foot apart. Be SURE these strings are exactly the same length. Tie the longer string between two chair backs.

Hold one ball still and start the other swinging back and forth by a push with your hand. Let go of the first ball. As the moving one begins to slow down, the other ball starts to swing back and forth. When it stops, the first one begins swinging again.

This experiment is a good way to see what is meant by

"sympathetic vibration." Sound waves have a certain "frequency" and every object in the world has its own natural frequency. When sound waves of a certain frequency strike an object that has the same frequency, they make it vibrate. This experiment shows how it works, but it is a sympathetic frequency of motion, not of sound.

The vibration of the first ball is carried along the overhead string to the second ball, which has the same rate of vibration as that carried to it.

THE BULL ROARER

How much noise can a six-inch wooden ruler make? Not very much, if you only strike it on a table or drop it on the floor. But try this.

Make a hole in the center of one end of a six-inch ruler and tie one end of a string through it. Tie the other end of the string to a short stick.

Now swing the stick as fast as you can around your head. Where is all that noise coming from?

As the ruler is swung, the air currents around it make it spin. It gives out a roaring sound as it sets the air in vibration.

THE SINGING WHEEL

Take a large flat coat button, a piece of string, and a piece of cardboard about four inches across.

Cut a circle from the cardboard, and make notches around the outside edge. Punch two holes in the center to match the two holes in the button.

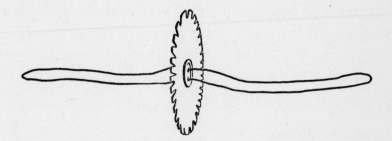

Now string the thread through the button, one length going through one hole, then through one hole in the cardboard. Bring the string back, stringing it through the other holes in the button and cardboard this time. Move the cardboard and button until they are in the middle of the string.

Make a loop at each end of the double string to hold it. Take one loop in each hand, and swing the button and cardboard wheel around in a circle like you swing a jump rope. This winds up the wheel.

As the wheel begins to unwind, and while it is spinning rapidly, pull gently on the loops in the string. This makes the wheel wind and unwind.

Hold the "teeth" of the wheel against the edge of a playing card or stiff cardboard, and it will sing for you.

Notice that the sound changes as the wheel goes faster or slower. Differences in the "pitch" of sound depend on the speed of vibration.

MUSIC FROM BOTTLES

Do you know the notes of the musical scale—Do, Mi, Sol, Do? You can make a musical instrument that will play these notes.

You will need four small bottles with mouths one-half inch in diameter, a ruler, and some sticky tape.

With the tape, fasten the bottles in a row to the ruler. Now put water in them. Fill the first one almost full, put less in the second and third, and leave the last one almost empty.

Blow across the mouth of the bottles. Each one gives out a different note. By adding or pouring out water, you can tune the bottles to the musical notes, *Do, Mi, Sol, Do*. The difference in sound is caused by shortening the depth of the air column in the bottle.

Can you play a tune on them?

6. The World of Light

SHUT your eyes for a moment. Everything is black.

Now open your eyes. The room is just as it was before. Why did it disappear when you shut your eyes?

When you shut your eyes, you shut out the light. Without light, our eyes cannot see anything. We do not really see THINGS, even with our eyes open. We see light reflected from things. If this is hard to believe, shut your eyes again.

Our eyes are the windows through which we see light, and unless we have light, we cannot see.

Light travels in waves, just as sound does. Light waves travel so fast that we say "as fast as light" when we mean so fast that it cannot be measured. Look at the brightest thing in the room with you. Before you could see it, the light waves had to travel from it to your eyes. How long did that take?

Scientists know how fast light waves travel. They go 186,000 miles in ONE SECOND. If we could make a jet rocket that could travel as fast as light, it would go around the world seven and one-half times in ONE second.

Light looks as if it is white or pale yellow. When you look at the light from the sun, can you believe that it is actually made up of all the colors we know?

You can prove this by looking outside on a bright moon-light night. Even though it may seem almost as bright as day, all of the colors we know are gone. Everything is a different shade of gray.

When your mother buys clothes, she sometimes takes them to a window to see what their real color is. Things look different in different kinds of light.

If you have seen a rainbow, you have seen the colors of sunlight. They are red, orange, yellow, green, blue, indigo, violet. You can remember these colors in the right order by learning this sentence: "Read over your good book in verse." The first letter of each word in the sentence is the first letter of a color in the rainbow.

Each color of light wave has a different length, red light waves are the longest, and violet the shortest. There are colors that we cannot see, just as there are sounds we cannot hear. The color waves that are too long for us to see we call "infrared" and those too short for us to see we call "ultraviolet."

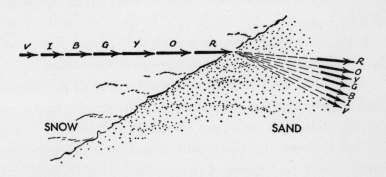

Suppose that seven boys had seven sleds, and each sled was a different length, just as light waves are. The red sled would be longest, then the orange, the yellow, green, blue, indigo, and finally the violet, which would be shortest. If the sleds all started down a hill at the same time, and went across a dirt road at an angle, each sled would cross the road in a different path. The longest sled would change its direction the least as it hit the dirt road, the shortest would change the most.

This is what happens to make a rainbow. The light waves are bent sharply as they hit small water drops in the air, and each takes a separate path, so each can be seen alone.

When sunlight strikes something red, only the red light waves are reflected. All the others are absorbed.

The paper of this book looks white, so it seems that it has no color at all. This is because it reflects *all* light rays. Black things reflect no light, but absorb all light rays. White light is made up of all colors, black is the absence of color.

What do you see when you look in a mirror? We are so used to looking at ourselves in mirrors that we think we see ourselves just as we are. If you want to see what a mirror really does, hold up this page in front of one.

The printing is backward. A mirror reverses light rays, or makes them look backward. Try this trick—print the word TOOT on a piece of paper and hold it in front of a mirror. It will look the same in the mirror as it does on the paper. Can you think of any other words that will do this? These letters, A H I M O T U V W X Y look the same on paper and in a mirror.

All smooth shiny surfaces will reflect light. Have you ever looked at a pond, and seen trees and grass reflected? Hold a glass of water over your head, and you will see that the underside of the surface of water makes a good mirror, too.

We put glass windows in our homes because glass lets

light waves through. We say that glass is transparent. Did you ever see light rays reflect back from a window, instead of going through it? When light rays strike a smooth surface at a certain angle, they are reflected back.

Sometimes you can see through the water in a pond all the way to the bottom. Other days, you can't see anything but the top of the water. When light is reflected back from the inner surface of any transparent material, it is called "internal reflection."

Water seems to bend light rays. Put a pencil in a glass of water, and look at the glass from one side. It looks as if the part of the pencil under water had moved over. The pencil is still just the same, but the way it looks is caused by "refraction."

When light goes from air into water (or any transparent material) its speed is changed. The light waves that go straight against the surface keep going without changing direction. The light waves that are at an angle change direction a little bit.

Here is a way to see this. If you slid on your sled down a hill at an angle, across a dirt path, and on to snow again, your sled would change its direction. When you crossed the dirt, it would change, and when it got to the snow it would change again. One of your runners would reach the dirt a little bit ahead of the other, and would slow down. This would change the way you were going. The same thing would happen when the sled hit the snow again—the first runner to get on the snow would go faster than the one still on the dirt.

This is what happens to light rays when they enter water. They are bent, and we call it refraction.

Some kinds of refraction make things look larger. We see this in a magnifying glass. When light passes through a curved surface, the rays of light are bent to make things seem bigger than they are. The glass in a microscope or telescope or magnifying glass is curved to bend the light rays in this special way.

A very long time ago, before men knew how to shape glass for this use, they used a drop of water instead. We are told that they made a small round frame of metal or wood and carefully put one drop of water inside it. The water took the shape of a ball. If you would like to try this, use a piece of waterproof paper. It is hard to do, and you cannot see very well through the water.

Through care and patience scientists have learned a great deal but there is still much that we do not know about light. This makes it one of the most interesting things in our world. Most of our light comes from the sun; it lets us see, helps plants to grow, and is a form of energy. We have batteries that run on energy from sunlight, called "solar" batteries. We have houses that are heated all year just from sunlight.

There is enough energy in the sunlight that falls on the earth to run every machine and heat every building on earth. If we knew more about how to use it, we could raise much more food and live better lives.

Someone will discover these other secrets of light. If you want to help, here are some experiments to start you on your way.

Light Plays Tricks on Our Eyes

There is a great deal of difference between the color black, and the color of silver. You can make something that is VERY black look like shiny silver.

You will need a candle, a small glass bottle, a glass of water, and a pair of tweezers.

Hold the bottle in the tweezers, put it in the yellow part of the candle flame. It will very quickly become covered with soot. Let it cool and then drop it gently into the glass of water. Instead of being black, it is now shiny silver-colored.

How did light play this trick on our eyes? When we talked about the surface tension of water, we learned about adhesion and cohesion. Some molecules of different things attract each other, and we call it adhesion.

The molecules of water and carbon have almost no adhesion. Because of this, a surface of water was formed where the carbon on the outside of the bottle touched the water. This surface reflected light rays, just as any surface of a transparent material will.

How to Bend Light

Put a pencil in a glass of water so that part of it sticks out above the water. Look at it from the side. It looks as if the pencil had moved to one side where it enters the water.

Look at it from above the water line, but to one side, and you will see parts of two pencils. Every time you change the direction from which you look, you see something different.

This is proof that we do not see *things* but the light rays reflected from them. The pencil has not changed a bit, but when the reflected light left the water the increase in speed caused it to "bend." What you saw was the result of this refraction of light rays by water.

What Curved Water Does to Light Rays

Collect as many odd-shaped bottles of clear glass as you can find. Fill them with water. The water will take the exact shape of the inside of the bottle and make a "water lens."

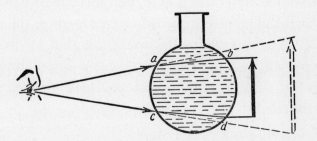

A bottle that is spherical, or shaped like a ball, will make a magnifying glass. The spot where the magnifying is clear and not distorted will probably be small, but you can see how much larger it makes things look. Other bottles of different shapes will make things look very odd. When you look at a mirror in a Fun House in an amusement park, the glass of the mirror has been curved so it will give a reflection that is out of shape. Different-shaped bottles will do something like this.

An Experiment with Diffusion

Clear cellophane seems completely without color. You can make it look white very easily.

Take a piece of clear cellophane and crumple it in your hand. Shape it into a ball.

Now look at it. It looks white. If you unfold it and smooth out all the wrinkles you can, it is not quite as clear as it was before.

You did not change the cellophane into something else by crumpling it, and you certainly did not color it. You broke the surface into many tiny angles that would reflect light, instead of letting it pass through.

Hold the cellophane in your hand and turn it from side to side. You can see the light reflected back from each wrinkle. If you could take all of the wrinkles out, it would be as clear and colorless as before.

One Color Can Make Us See Another

Put a piece of colored cellophane over a flashlight and turn its beams on to white paper. The color you see will be the color of the cellophane you have put over the light. Stare at the spot of colored light for a minute. Now turn off the flashlight, but keep looking at the same spot. If the cellophane was red you will see blue-green, if blue-green you will see red, and if it was yellow you will see blue. These pairs of colors are called complementary colors.

Sometimes our eyes get tired of looking at one color, and this experiment shows us what can happen. They suddenly see its complementary color.

MULTIPLE REFLECTIONS

You know that there is only one of you, and yet light rays can multiply you.

You will need two or three mirrors that you can stand up on a table top or desk. Arrange them so that when you look in one mirror, you can see yourself in the others. As you look, you see yourself multiplied over and over. How many "you's" can you see?

HOW TO MAKE A RAINBOW

Usually we see a rainbow after a storm, when small drops in the air refract beams of sunlight.

Sometimes we see rainbows in pools of water when a thin film of oil is on their surface. The colors are the same, whether we see the rainbow in the sky or reflected from oil on water.

You can make a rainbow by dropping a few drops of castor oil in a shallow bowl of water. The castor oil will spread in a thin film. Look at it from different angles and you will find the rainbow you have made.

You Can Mix Colored Light

It is hard to believe that all colors mixed together make white, but you can prove it with this experiment.

Cut several circles about six or eight inches in diameter from stiff cardboard. Mark them in sections as if you were cutting a pie in pieces.

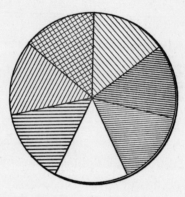

On one circle you will want seven of these sections, each section one color of the rainbow. You can color them with crayons, but it is better to cut colored paper and glue it on.

On another circle, make one section red, the next green, and so on around the circle. On another, use blue and green in the same way.

Make a hole in the center of each circle large enough for a pencil to go through. Put one circle at a time on a pencil and spin it as fast as you can. What do you see when you look at it?

COLORED LIGHT CHANGES COLORS

You can see how colored light changes the way colors look by using a flashlight with different colors of cellophane to put over it. Make crayon marks of every different color you have on a piece of white paper. Look at them with red cellophane over the flashlight, then green, then any color you like. Each time your crayon marks look different.

LIGHT CHANGED TO HEAT

You will need two milk bottles and two balloons. Blacken one bottle with soot from a candle flame. Leave the other one clean and bright.

Fasten a balloon over the mouth of each bottle, and set them in the sun. The balloon on the blackened bottle is blown up much faster than the other.

A strange thing about colors is the way they help change light to heat. When light waves can pass through a clear surface, they do not heat it very much. When they are absorbed by a dark surface, they turn to heat.

The heat from light rays absorbed by the blackened bottle makes the air inside the bottle expand, as air does when it is warmed. As it expands, it takes up more space and so moves into the balloon and blows it up.

7. The World of Heat

When we think of heat, we think of the hot sun in the summer, or a burning fire. Heat is important to us, because we are "warm-blooded animals" and we would rather be warm than cold.

Do you know what is the most important heat in our world to us? It is the heat in our own bodies. Without this heat, we could not live. Even on very cold days, when we play outside in the snow, our bodies stay warm.

Most of us keep our homes warm with fire. It may be the fire in a furnace or in a stove, and it may be made by burning wood or coal or gas.

Our bodies are kept warm by fire, too. We are made in such a wonderful way that the food we eat is burned by the oxygen in the air that we breathe.

When the weather gets cool, we put on extra clothing to keep warm. We often say that we are wearing a "warm" coat or sweater, but if you feel them you can tell that they are not warm. Coats and sweaters are only to keep our own body heat from going away into the air.

Heat, like light and sound, travels in waves. It moves out away from whatever is warm. Heat can go through some things very easily, and not so easily through others.

Materials that keep heat from going through are called "insulators." We use clothing to insulate our bodies, just as builders use different materials to insulate houses.

Heat is always making some kind of motion. Heat travels in three different ways, and heat makes changes in whatever gets warm.

Did you ever hold your hand near a pan in which food was cooking? You could feel the heat from the pan. You know that the food inside the pan is hot, and the pan is hot. This is what happens to something when it gets hot.

The molecules that make up the pan are very close together, because the pan is the "solid" form of metal. (If the pan were heated enough, the metal would become liquid, but this does not happen with heat from a stove.) As the pan begins to warm, the molecules move around, faster and faster, and get further apart. You cannot notice the change, but a hot pan is actually larger than a cold one because of this. If air or water is heated, it takes up a great deal more space, but most solids do not get very much larger from heat.

The heat coming out from the pan travels in heat waves. As they hit your hand, you feel them, and your hand becomes warmer. This is the kind of warmth you get from standing in front of a hot fire. It is called "radiant" heating, because the heat waves are radiating out from something warm.

As the heat waves go through the air, they warm the air. The warmer air is, the lighter it is. Light air is being pushed up by colder air, and floats on it, the way oil floats on water.

When men learned this about air they used the idea to heat houses. You can surprise your father by asking him if your home is warmed by "convection" heating. Convection heating means that air is heated, perhaps in the basement of a house, and rises up through pipes to open registers. As the hot air comes out of the registers, it keeps rising, and cold air moves down. This air is warmed and rises, and soon all of the air in the house is warm.

There is a third way heat travels. Did you ever use a metal spoon to stir something hot? Heat travels very fast through the molecules of metal, and the handle of the spoon may have gotten so hot that it burned you. As the molecules in the spoon got warm and moved about, they hit other molecules and passed some of the heat energy to them, so they became hot. Metal carries heat by conduction very fast, but wood and some plastics carry it much slower. This is why most spoons and knives and forks used for cooking have wood or plastic handles.

When something is very hot a strange thing happens to the heat waves it gives off. Heat waves are very short— it would take 250 of the longest ones to make 1 inch, and about 25,000 of the shortest ones to make an inch. An inch is this long ——————, so you can imagine just how short heat waves are.

When heat waves become *very* short, they turn to light waves. This is what makes electric light bulbs give off light. Inside a light bulb are some tiny wires, heated until they send out light waves. They still give out heat waves, as you can tell by holding your hand close to a light bulb.

If you hold a needle in a pair of tweezers and put one end of it in a candle flame, you can see this happen. As the tip of the needle gets hot, it turns red. As it gets still hotter, it gets to what we call "white" hot. It is now giving off light waves as well as heat waves.

Sound waves can be reflected and sent back as echoes, light waves are reflected by many things, and heat waves can also be reflected. Did you ever look inside a thermos bottle? The inside is very bright and shiny. When you put something hot in the thermos, the shiny inside reflects the heat waves back.

We may say that nothing stops convection better than something. That sounds silly, but when we say nothing we mean a vacuum, or a place without air. Without air, there are no convection currents to carry the heat across the empty space. Outside the shiny inside of the Thermos bottle is a vacuum. If any heat should get through the shiny inside, there would be no convection currents to carry it through this vacuum.

We talked about insulating to stop heat from escaping. The vacuum bottle also has insulation. This is why a vacuum bottle works so well—it uses reflection, a vacuum, and insulation!

You can't feel color, but color makes a difference in the way heat travels. Did you ever notice that most heating stoves are black? This is because a dull black surface radiates heat very fast.

In summer we wear white clothes to keep cool. When heat waves from the sun strike something white, they are reflected back.

We know when we are too hot to feel comfortable, or too cold to feel comfortable. We can only measure exactly how hot or how cold something is by using a thermometer. Until thermometers were invented, men could only guess the temperature. Now we can measure heat from 459 degrees below zero to thousands of degrees above! Your doctor uses a thermometer to tell when you have a fever. A fever means that your body heat has risen from 98.6 degrees to something higher, and shows that your body is fighting some kind of germ.

The thermometers we know best are called Fahrenheit thermometers, because they were invented by a Mr. Fahrenheit.

We call 32 degrees the freezing point, because water will freeze when it is that cold. Zero on the Fahrenheit was the point Mr. Fahrenheit believed was the temperature of salt and ice. The real zero point, or temperature at which the action of molecules is believed to stop completely, is 459 degrees *below* this zero.

Heat does many jobs in our world. If our bodies were not kept warm by the food we eat, we would die. If eggs were not kept warm by the heat from the mother's body, they could not hatch. Seeds could not sprout, plants could not grow, the air in our world would not move, without heat.

Here are some experiments you can do to learn more about it:

Why We Need Thermometers

We know when we are either too warm or too cold to be comfortable. We can tell whether one thing is warmer than another, just by feeling both things.

This way of measuring heat is by comparing one temperature with another. It is not a very exact way.

If you want to prove this, you will need three bowls of water. One should be hot, one very cold, and the other lukewarm.

Put one hand in the hot water and the other in the cold water. Let them stay a minute or two, and put both hands in the bowl of lukewarm water.

To the hand that was in hot water, the lukewarm water feels cool. To the hand that was in cold water, it seems warm. Only a thermometer can tell us just what temperature it is.

How Heat Can Separate Molecules

When some solids are mixed with water, they make a solution. The molecules of the solid divide and go into the spaces between the molecules of the water. The solid seems to have disappeared, but you can take it out again.

Stir salt into a pan of water until the water will hold no more, and the salt is completely dissolved.

Put the pan of water on the stove and slowly bring it to a boil. Let it boil gently, and you will see the water getting less and less. The water molecules are going into the air as water vapor.

When the water has all evaporated, the salt that you stirred in it will be left. You have taken the salt out of the water.

How to Distill Water

When you distill water, you change it into water vapor, and then back to liquid water again. When water is distilled, any solids or impurities that were in it are taken out. They do not go into the air as vapor, so when the vapor turns into liquid water again it is pure. We use distilled water in our car batteries, and in some steam irons.

Here is an easy way for you to distill water with heat. Put some water in a teakettle and set it on top of the stove. Put a teacup over the spout of the teakettle and tie it to the handle of the teakettle. Set a shallow pan just under the teacup.

Now heat the water in the teakettle. As it heats, water vapor comes from the spout, condenses when it hits the cooler teacup, and falls in drops into the pan.

How Hot Air Can Make Things Move

Because cold air is heavier than warm, it pushes hot air upward. Anything that moves has force, and this force can be used to make other things move.

You will need a table lamp, a four-inch square of writing paper, a button, a piece of thread, and a needle.

Cut a pinwheel, and put the button on one end of the thread. Thread the needle with the other end of the thread, and put it through the points of the pinwheel.

Hang the pinwheel, or hold it, above the lamp. As the hot air touches it, it begins to turn. The moving hot air pushes the "wings" on the pinwheel and makes it turn, just as you can make a pinwheel turn by holding it in the wind.

What Black Does to Heat

Get a big cookie tin to set your equipment on, or do this experiment on the drainboard of the sink. You will need two small empty tin cans, like sardine cans, two pieces of crayon, and a candle.

Clean the bottom of one tin can until it is very shiny, and blacken the other in the candle flame.

Fasten a piece of crayon to the inside of the bottom of

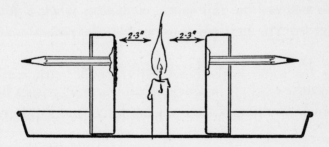

each tin can by a few drops of melted candle wax. (You will remember doing this to hold candles in place in earlier experiments.)

Set the cans up on end about two or three inches apart, with the bottoms facing each other.

Set the candle between the two tin cans, and be sure each can is the same distance away from it. Do not have them close enough that the candle flame can be blown against the can.

Light the candle. Notice which crayon falls off first.

This is because the blackened surface absorbed heat from the candle flame and became hot enough to melt the wax.

The shiny tin can reflected the heat back and stayed cooler.

How to Put Water in an Upside-Down Bottle

When water changes from hot to cool, it can do interesting things. For instance it can put water into a bottle that is upside down.

You will need a milk bottle, a shallow bowl, and some hot water. The best place to do this experiment is at the sink.

Put the water in the bowl. Fill the milk bottle with hot water (not hot enough to burn you) and then pour it out. Set the bottle quickly in the bowl of water, mouth down.

The water from the bowl rises up inside the bottle.

When you heated the milk bottle with hot water the air molecules in it became warmer. They spread out and took up more space. When you set the empty bottle in the water, the air began to cool, and the molecules rushed closer together. They took up less space, and the water rushed in to fill the space they had left.

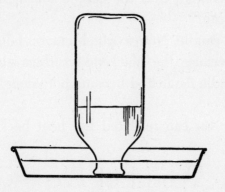

OTHER EXPERIMENTS

If you will look backward through this book, you will find other experiments that show you things heat can do. You might want to do them over, this time watching for the way heat acts.

Here are some of them. How many others can you find?

Wet- and dry-bulb thermometers.

How heat can sail a boat.

Blowing up a balloon with a milk bottle.

Breaking rubber with a milk bottle.

8. The World of Electricity

ELECTRICITY is one of the most exciting things in our world. It can be as fierce as a bolt of lightning that blasts a tree to pieces, or as gentle as the heat in your electric blanket. Many times it is dangerous, and yet certain kinds you can make yourself.

Scientists know a great deal about electricity but we can only tell you a little about it here. The more they know, the more they discover that they do not know.

Electricity is a kind of force, or energy. It gives us heat, light, cold, motion, sound, pictures and many other things. We cook food and heat our houses with it, make night almost as bright as day with it, cool our food and freeze ice cream with it, and ride in cars and boats and airplanes because of it. Our radios, phonographs, television sets and movies use it. It would be hard to imagine our world without it.

One kind of electricity was discovered more than twenty-five hundred years ago, but men did not learn how to use it until about one hundred years ago.

Most of you have heard about magnets and magnetism. Magnetism and electricity have certain things in common. No one knows who was the first man to discover magnetism. Perhaps a shepherd walking in a field hundreds of years before Christ was born, was carrying an iron rod, and suddenly felt it pulled downward toward the earth. Just under the surface of the earth was a large black stone. This stone, he saw, could pull iron toward it.

If you have a magnet, you have seen this happen. This is what goes on inside the iron to make it happen. If you throw a handful of beans on a table, they land every which way. Now if you straighten them out and put them in lines, they look very orderly.

The molecules of iron are like the beans that are every which way. When iron becomes magnetized, the molecules line up in regular rows. Each molecule has two different poles—one at each end. When they are lined up by magnetism, the like poles are all in one direction. This causes the piece of iron to have two kinds of poles, one kind at one end, and the other kind at the other end.

In a magnet, these poles are called the North Magnetic Pole and the South Magnetic Pole. This is because a magnetized bar of metal, when it is hung by a thread tied in its center, will turn until one pole points toward the north, and the other toward the south.

If you have two long magnets, watch what they do. Their two south poles push away from each other, and the two north poles do the same thing. If you put a north pole of one magnet close to a south pole of another magnet, they will pull each other. Like poles repel each other, or push away, and unlike poles attract each other, or pull each other.

Our earth has a North Pole and a South Pole. It also has a "Magnetic North Pole" and a "Magnetic South Pole" which we can find by using a compass. When the points of a compass point to the magnetic poles, they are not pointing to the geographic poles.

The magnetic pole in the north is called the "South Magnetic Pole" and is about eleven hundred miles away from the geographic North Pole. The magnetic pole in the south is called the "North Magnetic Pole" and is about the same distance from the geographic South Pole. The north pole of a compass needle is attracted by the "South Mag-

netic Pole" and points in that direction. The south pole of
the compass needle is attracted by the "North Magnetic
Pole" and points in that direction.

After men had begun to learn about the wonders of the
magnet, they invented a way to use it to guide ships on
the ocean. On dark days and starless nights, a magnet
could help them find their way. Very long ago, men used
magnets to make the first compasses. These men magnetized a small strip of steel, suspended it from a thread,
and saw by the points which way was north and which
south.

Men knew this much one thousand years ago, but they
did not know that the magnetic north and south poles are
not where the others are. This means that the magnetic
needle does not always point exactly to north or south.
When Columbus sailed to America, he saw that his compass needle pointed toward the northwest instead of true
north. This frightened his sailors, because they thought
their compass needle could no longer guide them home.

One end of a magnetic needle hanging from a thread is
pulled downward. The nearer it is to one of the magnetic
poles of the earth, the more it is pulled downward. When
it is exactly over the North Magnetic Pole, the South Pole
of a magnet will point straight down.

Our airplanes have magnetic detectors that are like these
dipping needles. When the plane flies over an ocean, the

iron and steel in a submarine under the water will pull one end of the needle down toward it and show the pilot of the airplane where the submarine is.

Two metals, nickel and cobalt, can only be magnetized slightly. Strangely enough, when these metals are mixed with different amounts of aluminum and copper (which cannot be magnetized at all), and iron, they make the very strongest magnets. These are alnico magnets.

The only other metal which can be magnetized is gadolinium.

About the same time that men discovered magnetic stones, other men discovered something just as strange. They found that amber, which is tree gum or resin turned to a fossil, when it was rubbed with fur or cloth, acted like a magnet. It would attract only very light things, like tiny bits of paper or straw.

This discovery was something new and different. We call it "static electricity." Static means still, or not moving.

You might think that when men learned this much about a new kind of force, they would have been very excited. When we discover something like this today, we start to find ways to make it work for us. At that time, men were not what we call "science-minded," in other words, they did not think like scientists. Most work was done by people or animals or perhaps the force of moving water. No one had ever thought that other things could be used instead.

People did tricks with static electricity, as we do card

tricks today. They thought it was amusing and interesting. It was nearly twenty-two hundred years before anyone did anything more about it.

When the first Queen Elizabeth ruled England, about four hundred years ago, her physician, William Gilbert, found that other things besides amber could be electrified. Gilbert called this force "electric" after *elektron,* the Greek word for amber.

The scientific age was starting, and men went to work with eager minds to learn more about this strange thing. At first they thought there were two kinds of electricity, because they discovered the push and the pull of this force. We know much more now than they did about what was happening in these early experiments. We know something about the atom that would have amazed them.

The atom is so tiny that for a long time men thought it was the smallest thing in the world. Now we know that even atoms, tiny as they are, are made up of things even smaller. Two of these are protons and electrons.

An atom is held together because the different parts of it are charged with electricity. The electrons have a negative charge, the protons have a positive charge. The atom is very much like our solar system, with the negative electrons moving around the core or center of the atom. This core contains all the protons. The continual attracting and repelling (or pushing and pulling) of these parts of the atom hold it together.

The various kinds of atoms in our world differ because each has a different number of protons and electrons. By changing this number, one kind of atom can be turned into another. An atom of mercury can be changed to an atom of gold. The mercury atom has 80 electrons and 80 protons, the gold atom only 79 of each. Scientists finally found that by the use of a terrific amount of force they could blast off one electron and one proton from the mercury atom and by doing so change it to gold. So far, this is so expensive that making gold in this way is not worth while.

By upsetting the balance of force inside an atom, we can now make new atoms, or man-made elements. When we get this far in science, we begin to find out how much we do not know. We have come a long way on our road to knowledge since man first discovered electricity, but only far enough to realize how long the road is.

The surface, or outside, of every body (and remember that in science the word body means an object) has an endless number of electrons that are not tied up in atomic structure. Think of a house in which a number of different people live, each busy doing his job—and outside this house are thousands of other people. These thousands outside are just like part of the people inside, but they are not doing the work of the house.

The number of these "free" electrons on the surface of a body determine whether it is neutral, charged with negative electricity, or charged with positive electricity. When it is neutral, there are neither too few or too many negative electrons on its surface. When it is negatively charged, it has an oversupply of electrons; when it is positively charged, it has too few.

This sounds very complicated, but this is what we believe happens when a piece of wool cloth is rubbed over a piece of plastic or hard rubber. This rubbing takes negative electrons from the cloth and puts them on the rubber. This charges the rubber with negative static electricity, and leaves the wool with a positive charge.

If you rub a glass bottle with a piece of silk, the negative electrons are taken from the glass and collect on the silk. The glass is positively charged, and the silk is negatively charged.

Static electricity seems to be an accumulation of these "free" negative electrons that are always ready to "jump" to a surface that has a shortage of them. A surface that has too few electrons is positive.

Now we can begin to see why two things charged with negative static electricity repel each other. The free electrons of the negative charge want to go toward a place that has too few—they cannot go toward a place that already has too many. When something with a positive charge is brought close to something with a negative charge, the free electrons have a place to jump and the two things attract each other.

Another queer thing that electrons on a charged body

do is to gather around any sharp point on it. In one of our experiments, you will see how this works, and find out why we have lightning rods on houses.

A magnet, and this is one of the great mysteries of science, acts in the same way, but it seems to have nothing to do with free electrons. A magnet has no static electricity.

The electricity that we use most is called "current" electricity. This is the kind that runs our electrical appliances. Current electricity is a stream of electrons flowing through a conductor. A conductor is a material through which electricity can move quickly and easily. A non-conductor is something through which electricity cannot move.

To make electricity we must gather free electrons and separate them from positive surfaces, to which they are attracted. Static electricity can be made by simply rubbing two bodies together, like cloth on hard rubber. It is called static because it stays in one place until it is discharged. Static electricity can be very strong and dangerous—lightning is static electricity—but it does not last very long. The free electrons leave one surface for another very quickly.

To make current electricity, which does so much work for us, we must gather many more electrons and separate them from positive surfaces. Then they flow through wire, which is a very good conductor. They always flow from a negative charge to a positive charge.

This is what makes them move. In the mass of gathered

electrons, each electron repels every other electron. At the same time they are pulled toward the positively charged end of the conductor. This push and pull makes them flow very fast. Electrons flowing from a negative charge to a positive one are called "direct" current. Oddly enough, electricity can be made to flow back and forth through the same wire, and this is called "alternating" current. The names we usually use are DC for direct current, and AC for alternating current.

When you have read this, you know more about electricity than men knew for twenty-two hundred years after it had been discovered.

How to Make a Compass

A long time ago, men who sailed ships on the ocean did not carry a compass. When they needed one to find out which direction to sail, they made one. You can do the same thing.

You will need a small magnet, a needle, a piece of paper, a string, a plastic Thermos bottle top, a plastic cap from a tube of toothpaste, and a cork. With this material, you can make two different compasses.

First, cut a small triangle of paper and tie a thread to one point. Hang this in a doorway, or from a chair back, so it can swing freely.

Rub your magnet on the needle, rubbing only in one direction. Put the needle through the triangle of paper.

The needle swings until one end is pointing toward the Magnetic North Pole and one toward the Magnetic South Pole.

For another kind of compass, fill the plastic Thermos bottle top with water. You can either rest the cap from the tube of toothpaste on the water and fasten the magnetized

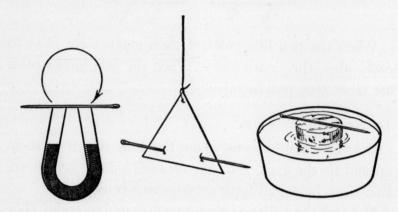

needle to it with sticky tape, or put the cork on the water, and rest the needle on it. The needle must rest on something which will float freely in the water. The needle will turn until it shows you north and south.

How Magnetism Pushes and Pulls

Magnetism is like electricity in several ways. Magnetized objects have two poles and like poles repel, unlike poles attract.

To see this you will need two small bar magnets, and four round toothpicks or kitchen matches. If you use matches, take the heads off before you begin this experiment.

Set two toothpicks (or matches) under each magnet like rollers. Put them close together, and see what happens.

When the two like poles of each magnet are close to each other, they push away. When the two unlike poles are close, they pull together.

Tricks with Balloons

Get two small balloons, about the same size. Blow them up and tie the ends. Rub one on each side of your head. Rub them back and forth on your hair briskly.

Now set the balloons close together on the table. They push each other away, because each has a negative charge. This charges goes away very quickly, but you can put it back again by rubbing it over your hair again.

Put a pinch of salt or sugar on the table. Rub one of the balloons against briskly over your hair, and hold it close to the salt or sugar. Hear the tiny "pings" as it picks up the salt!

How to Make a Different Kind of Static Electricity

Rubbing fur or wool (or hair) on things like hard rubber or plastic makes a charge of negative static electricity. You

can make a positive charge by rubbing a piece of silk or
nylon over glass. Charge a small glass bottle this way, and
a plastic comb with a piece of wool cloth. Experiment and
see what they do when brought close together.

TRICKS WITH STATIC ELECTRICITY

This experiment will work better on a cool dry day than
on a warm damp one. When the air is damp, electrons will
go off into the air more quickly than when it is dry and
cool. The faster electrons go into the air, the less static
electricity you can create.

If you walk across a wool rug on a cool day, rubbing
your feet as you walk, you charge your body with negative
static electricity. Then if you touch a water faucet or a
metal radiator right after you do this, you will feel a little
electric "shock." This is the electricity leaving your body
and going into the metal. If you do this in a dark room, you
can see a spark jump from your finger to the metal.

Do it again, but carry a piece of metal with a sharp
point, like a needle, in your hand. Touch the water faucet
or radiator with the needle, and you will feel no shock.
The metal acted as a lightning rod, and carried the electricity away without shocking you.

The lightning rods on top of our houses carry the static
electricity through a wire to the ground.

Some people seem to pick up more of a static electricity
charge than others. When they have ridden in a car for a

long time, they get a shock when they touch the metal car door. These people can avoid the shock by touching the door with the car key instead of with their hands.

Rub a piece of paper with a piece of wool, and put it on a windowpane. It will stick to the pane. The paper had a negative charge, the glass had a positive one.

How to Make an Electricity Detective

One of the many things we do not know about electricity is just why some charges are positive and some are negative. We know that usually when an animal material, like fur or wool or hair, is rubbed over certain substances, a negative charge is made. When silk or nylon is rubbed over something like glass, a positive charge is made.

You can't see electricity, but you can find out whether something has a negative or a positive charge. To do this, you will need an electroscope. An electroscope is a scientific instrument which you can make.

You will need a small glass bottle, a foil chewing gum wrapper, a toothpick, and a paper clip. Bend out the paper clip so that each end makes a hook. Very carefully cut two tiny strips from the gum wrapper. With a needle, make a hole in the end of each one, large enough for the wire of the paper clip to go through. Soak the strips in warm water until the paper backing can be taken off without tearing the foil. You use this kind of foil because it is thinner than the aluminum foil your mother uses. Because it is thin, it will tear easily, so you must be careful.

Now slip the two foil strips over one hook on the paper clip, just a tiny bit apart.

Hang the other hook of the paper clip over the tooth-pick, and let it hang inside the bottle.

You are ready to be an electricity detective.

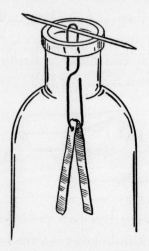

First, charge a balloon with negative static electricity. Touch it to the top of the paper clip. The foil strips spread apart because the negative charge made them repel each other.

Now charge something else with static electricity, bring it close to your electroscope. If the strips spread more, it was a negative charge. If the strips start to close, it was a positive charge.

How to Make a Flashlight

Flashlights are one way we use electricity. Electricity is the flow of free electrons and we can make electricity by finding a way to make them flow.

A battery is a little box of substances that can make a chemical change. This chemical change makes an electric current flow through the battery. The current will do many things, and one of them is to make a bulb light up.

Some flashlights have many pieces, but they all work the same way. You can make a flashlight from a small "pen" battery, a small flashlight bulb, and a gum wrapper.

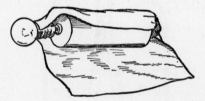

A flashlight battery has two poles—a negative and a positive. If it has a cardboard case, the bottom is the negative pole. If it does not, the metal outside is the negative pole. The little knob in the center of the top of the battery is the positive pole.

Lay the battery on the foil side of the gum wrapper, and set the bulb so that its tip will touch the positive pole of the battery. Now bend the foil so that it is touching the negative pole of the battery and the metal part of the bottom of the flashlight bulb. The bulb will light.

If you can find an old flashlight to take apart, you can see how it works. The spring in the bottom of the flashlight case makes a contact with the negative pole, carrying the negative charge up the side of the case. The tip of the bulb touches the tip of the positive pole of the battery. The button that turns the flashlight off or on completes the circuit, or breaks it, by moving a tiny piece of metal inside the case.

Now that you know this, here is a trick you can do. Put a metal ring on your finger, and hold a tiny flashlight battery inside your hand. Hold a bulb between your ring finger and the next one so that its tip touches the positive pole of the battery. Now, by practice, you can learn to make the ring complete the circuit between the negative pole of the battery and the metal part of the light bulb. The battery is so tiny no one can see it, and if you do the trick properly, it will look as if you can light a bulb by holding it between your fingers.

What a Battery Does to a Compass

You will need the "cork" compass you made before, a flashlight battery, and a piece of wire.

Fasten one end of the wire to the positive pole of the battery with tape, and the other end to the negative pole the same way. Be sure your wire is long enough so you will have room to work. Now lay the battery on the table, as in the picture, and set your compass on top of the wire.

The current from the battery, running through the wire, makes a magnetic field. The compass needle will point crosswise to the wire, proving this is true.

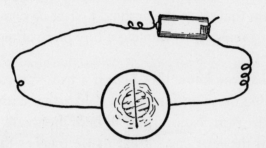

If you change the direction of the current by reversing the connections to the battery, the needle will turn around and point in the opposite direction.

Don't leave your battery hooked up this way very long, or you will wear it out.

How to Make an Electromagnet

This experiment will show you another way in which magnetism and electricity are alike. You can *make* a magnet that works by electricity.

You will need a flashlight battery, a length of covered wire (this is wire covered with thread or paint to insulate it and keep the electricity inside), and a nail.

Wind the middle section carefully around the nail.

Leave the two ends of the wire free. Now fasten them to the flashlight battery just as you did before. You have an electromagnet which will work as long as the battery has electricity in it.

This magnet will attract bits of iron like small tacks or paper clips, and will drop them as soon as you unfasten one end of the wire.

Some electromagnets are so strong that they will lift tons of iron.

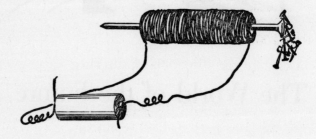

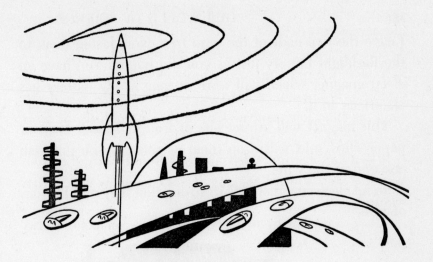

9. The World of the Future

Your trip into the world of science through this book is almost ended. We hope that you have enjoyed it, and that you feel like an explorer who has gone into new lands and found many new things. We hope, even more, that this is only your first trip and that some part of this book has interested you so much that you will decide to go further.

Do you know that what you have learned from this book is more than any one man knew about science even four hundred years ago?

Even the very simplest things that men have discovered

about our world have led to very wonderful inventions. When Benjamin Franklin flew a kite in an electrical storm, he found that lightning was a huge electric spark. This was the very beginning of learning to harness the wonderful force of electricity and making it do so much of the work of the world.

When men learned why rain falls from clouds, they took the first step toward making it rain or snow when they wanted it to.

When men began to understand how an echo works, they were on the way to inventing radar.

There is still so much for us to learn, and so much for us to do, that you have an unlimited field before you. Perhaps some small thing that you have learned from this book may help you make a discovery or invention that will change the whole world.

Think of all the things the world needs—a way to raise more food, new sources of power so everyone can have a better life, ways to cure disease, ways to make things grow where the soil is poor, peace for our whole world.

These are jobs that are waiting for you.

Science has never invented anything more wonderful than your mind, and there is nothing that you cannot do with it.

There are no more experiments in this book, but there are a million experiments in your mind, waiting for you to think of them.

Your trip with us is over, but you are starting on a new one that will last your whole life long. We hope that your big trip will be successful, and that our world will be even more wonderful because of you.

Index

207372